Echoes of the Ancient World

Series editor Werner Forman

viking
hammer of
the north

VIKING
hammer of the north

Magnus Magnusson

photographs by
Werner Forman

ORBIS PUBLISHING · London

NOTES ON PRONUNCIATION

In this book, Icelandic names are given in the original, apart from dropping the nominatival ending which is not a root part of the word itself. The Icelandic accents are also used, because they affect the pronunciation of vowels. Un-accented vowels are pronounced like English vowels, but accented vowels are pronounced as follows:

á as in *owl*
é (pronounced *ye*) as in *yet*
í as in *seen*
ó as in *note*
ö as in French *fleur*
ú as in *soon*
ý as in *fear*
ei as in *tray*
au as in French *oeil*
æ (a dipthong called 'ash'), as in *life*.

There are two extra consonants in Icelandic, the Old English ð (Ð), called 'eth' and pronounced *th* as in *breathe*; and the Old English þ (Þ), called 'thorn' and pronounced *th* as in *thin*.

© Orbis Publishing Limited, London 1976
Originally appeared as Hammer of the North
Myths and Heroes of the Viking Age
This edition first published 1979
2nd printing December, 1979
Printed in Czechoslovakia
ISBN 0 85613 301 9

Werner Forman and the publishers would like to acknowledge the help of the following museums and authorities in permitting the photography shown on the pages listed.

Århus Kunstmuseum, Denmark: 114 top.

The British Museum, London, England: 118 bottom.

City of London Guildhall Museum, England: 40–41.

Manx Museum, Isle of Man: 51.

Nationalmuseet, Copenhagen, Denmark: 13, 30–31, 41, 42–43, 46, 52 bottom, 56, 57, 63, 69, 76 bottom, 102–103, 106–107.

Silkeborg Museum, Denmark: 115.

Statens Historiska, Stockholm, Sweden: 6, 12, 16, 19, 20, 21, 22 left, 26 bottom, 29, 33, 36, 38 left, 50, 54–55, 59, 60, 61, 62, 64, 65, 70, 71 right, 72–73, 74, 75, 76 top, 78, 81 bottom, 83, 84–85, 88 left, 89, 90, 93, 96, 97, 99 top, 102, 108, 109, 112 top, 113, 117, 118 top, 125.

Stofnun Árna Magnússonar á Íslandi, Reykjavik, Iceland: 38 right, 39, 91.

Thjodminjasafn, Reykjavik, Iceland: 68, 71 left.

Universitetetsbiblioteket, Uppsala, Sweden: 47.

Universitetets I Bergen Historisk Museum, Norway: 26 top, 101.

Universitetets Oldsaksamling, Oslo, Norway: 17, 27 bottom, 120, 121, 122, 123.

Upplandsmuseet, Uppsala, Sweden: 22 right, 116.

Vikingskipene, Bygdoy, Norway: 24, 25, 32, 52 top, 53, 79, 81 top, 98–99, 112 bottom.

contents

Preface 7

The Land of Thule 9
Pre-Viking Scandinavia

The Dragon Ships 21
The great age of Viking expansion

Hammer and Cross 33
The coming of the new religion

The Great Void 43
Creation and doom in Viking cosmology

Óðin: the All-Father 55
Lord of the gallows and lord of the slain

Storm and Harvest 67
Thór, Frey, Freyja: gods of the earth and sky

Loki and Baldur 79
The father of lies and the shining god

Choosers of the Slain 87
Valkyries and the spirits of the Otherworld

The Way to Hel 95
Death and the after-life

Sacred Stones 105
Norsemen at worship

The Heroic Ethic 117
The legend of Sigurð and the code of the warrior

Bibliography 126

Index 126

A fine gilt-silver brooch from Gotland, made during the Migration Period. It gives a clear indication of the richness of pre-Viking Scandinavia

pReface

For many centuries, the Vikings were reviled as a race of cruel and bloodthirsty assassins, intent only on plundering the wealth of a serenely Christian Europe, delighting only in looting and rape and murder. By the monks of the medieval Church they were depicted as pagan devils, anti-Christ personified: men without religion or morality, who died as brutally and carelessly as they had lived. That was the Viking image – and it still lingers on in some of the books that are being written even to this day.

Modern scholarship, however, is gradually revealing a very different picture of the Vikings, or rather of the Scandinavians of the so-called 'Viking Age', as traders and explorers, settlers and poets, and as extraordinarily inventive artists. Viking mythology – the religion of Scandinavia from the Bronze Age to medieval times – has also been promoted from the level of fairy-tale and nursery stories.

In a turbulent age, when the Vikings with their superior naval technology and pent-up dynamism exploded from their homelands to extend the bounds of the known world, they appeared as a bolt from the blue – a thunderbolt from across the sea, the Hammer of the North. Thór's Hammer was a potent symbol of their strength, their daring, and their effectiveness.

In this book, I have tried to piece together a picture of what the Vikings and their ancestors believed in: their gods, their spirits, their forms of worship, their ethics. I have used the original literary sources of the Icelandic descendants of the Vikings, tempered with the discoveries of archaeology and the findings of anthropology. But inevitably, in the absence of contemporary records from the Vikings themselves, I have had to make subjective judgements about the nature and profundity of Viking religion and its formal expression in the heroic code of conduct. As fresh insights are gained, I am convinced that it will become ever more clear that the Vikings, far from being the mindless savage brutes of popular prejudice, were capable of an intellectually subtle and artistically sophisticated view of both this world and the next.

MAGNUS MAGNUSSON

the land
of thule
pre-viking scandinavia

The first recorded glimpses of Scandinavia are blurred and tantalizing. Around 330 BC, as Alexander the Great was setting out on his conquest of the East, a Greek explorer from Marseilles set out on a sea-voyage west and north round the coasts of Europe. His name was Pytheas. He was a mathematician, astronomer and navigator, and the purpose of his voyage, financed by the city fathers of Marseilles, seems to have been to explore the sea-routes to the tin and amber markets of northern Europe.

Not a word of his original narrative of this epic voyage, *On the Ocean*, survives. But it seems to have contained a wealth of observations and information about the relatively unknown lands of the north, which

Left Northern skies that beckon the traveller towards Thule. No one now knows what the name means: Thule was always somewhere just beyond the farthest known north

9

was quoted by later writers, albeit sceptically. It is clear that he visited Britain and the northern isles of Shetland and the Orkneys. He described the amber island of Abalus, now thought to have been Heligoland, whose inhabitants traded amber with the Teutones of Jutland. Pytheas seems also to have sailed far north up the western coast of Norway, to a land he called Thule, six days' sail north of Britain. It was a rainy, sunless place, where the inhabitants lived by agriculture. They grew millet, which they threshed in covered barns, and supplemented their diet with herbs, roots, and berries.

No one can now be sure where Pytheas' Thule lay, but it must have been far north of the Arctic Circle because the daylight in summer lasted 24 hours. It was the end of the inhabited world, beyond which stretched a primordial confusion of the elements: snow-clad mountains spouting fire, icebergs drifting in a boiling sea, and even farther on a sort of primeval jelly on which it was impossible to walk or to sail. It was neither water, air nor ice, but a mysterious substance which the explorers named 'the lung of the sea'. One day's sailing further to the north, the water was solid ice.

It is a great pity that the original account of Pytheas' expedition should have reached us in so garbled and distorted a form. Strabo of Pontus, three centuries later, made copious reference to Pytheas in his 17-volume *Geographica*, but was clearly prejudiced against him, and cited him chiefly to pour scorn on him. Pytheas, it now appears, must have been a meticulous observer as well as a courageous explorer. The confused descriptions of the far north attributed to him bear a telling resemblance to some of the northern geological phenomena familiar to us in the present day—submarine volcanic eruptions off the coast of Iceland, for instance. And now that the broad outlines of the story of prehistoric Scandinavia have been clarified, Pytheas has been vindicated.

The earliest inhabitants of Scandinavia, thousands of years before the time of Pytheas, were hunter-gatherers —nomadic tribes or clans who lived by hunting, fishing and bird-fowling and gathering whatever food grew wild. Their presence in Scandinavia first became apparent some 12,000 years ago, soon after the last ice age. Because they built no settlements, the archaeological traces they left are sporadic and fortuitous— occasional flints for arrows, knives or spears, bone tools and utensils, some skeletons in shallow graves. They left impressive examples of their art, however, carved on rock faces along the coasts of Norway—the art of the Arctic Stone Age. Some of the carvings are naturalistic, depicting huge figures of elks, bears and reindeer; others are stylized representations of birds, fish and weapons. There are scenes showing human figures in a dance, apparently wearing horned head-dresses, and these suggest magic rituals intended to expedite the hunt.

Somewhere around 3000 BC, agriculture was introduced into Scandinavia—probably about a thousand

years later than in Britain. It may have been brought by an immigrant people, or it may have developed indigenously. Its effect was gradually to replace the nomadic, hunting-gathering way of life by organized settlements of people who cleared the land of forests, planted crops, and domesticated livestock. It was only now that certain basic social organizations became possible; agricultural surpluses could support a degree of specialization through a division of labour and thus maintain a formal hierarchy based on the distribution of wealth. For the first time, large-scale community projects could be undertaken—in particular, the building of megalithic tombs in which whole families or clans were interred together, generation after generation. In addition to the specialist masons and builders, whom the community and its leaders could now afford to keep, forms of institutionalized religion could also be supported with priests either serving the chieftaincy or wielding authority in their own right as priest-chieftains. It is impossible to be precise about the beliefs or ceremonies involved; perhaps the great tombs were a kind of ever-present Otherworld in which the dead were thought to continue a life of their own. Certainly, the presence of the bones of the ancestors would give members of the community a strong sense of continuity, and a link with the spirit world they inhabited. It is reasonable to assume, from what little evidence there is, that ceremonial rites were associated with these megalithic tombs. They may have involved veneration of a Mother Earth goddess or other aspects of fertility, with the cycle of the seasons and of life and death.

The picture of Scandinavia that emerges throughout the third millennium BC, in the late Neolithic Age, is a comparatively tranquil one. But early in the second millennium Scandinavia was invaded by peoples from the south and south-east, known from their weapons as the Battle-Axe people. They are believed to have been

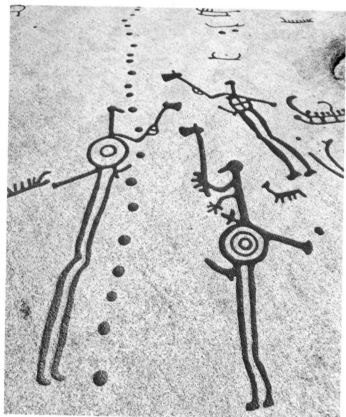

Apart from their evident mystery, Bronze Age rock carvings from Sweden reflect the growing Scandinavian preoccupation with virility and aggressive activity, and a new belief in personified gods.
Top left: Warriors and bull in an enigmatic hunting scene, associated with the disc of the sun.
Top right: Phallic figures on board a ship, apparently performing a ceremonial axe dance. The beaked stem and stern of the ship anticipate the longships of the Viking Age.
Above: Ceremonial confrontation with axes and phallus erect, associated with the sky-god. The disc of the sun is anthropomorphized to become warriors

Indo-European, and they brought with them new customs and beliefs that changed Scandinavian civilization profoundly.

The Battle-Axe people ushered in the Scandinavian Bronze Age, which is generally dated from about 1500 BC to 500 BC. Scandinavia was now open to foreign influences, by way of trade and travel. From the magnificent treasures that have been unearthed by archaeologists it is clear that this was an age of considerable new wealth and prosperity, particularly in Denmark where the amber of Jutland financed the importing of tin, copper and gold.

Scandinavia now had a new ruling warrior-caste whose dead were laid in thousands of imposing burial mounds, surrounded by their weapons and adornments. Their funeral chambers were also furnished with a mass of domestic goods and utensils that have miraculously survived the centuries, such as clothes and cups and chairs. The new preoccupations with power and the acquisition of wealth are also reflected in a complete change of style in the rock-carvings. Whereas in the Arctic Stone Age there had been naturalistic representations of animals of the hunt, the Bronze Age was remarkable for stylized representations of warriors wielding axes and spears and swords, of men dancing and ploughing, of phallic ceremonies. Everywhere the accent is on virility and aggressive action.

For the first time we can also detect clear evidence of a belief in personified gods, gods of the sky, gods of battle, gods of fertility. Those mighty armed figures with phallus erect, dwarfing the warriors about them, can only be interpreted as gods. There is a profusion of symbolic representations of the sun as a disc or wheel, sometimes alone, sometimes carried on a ship or drawn in a wagon. The ships themselves are fascinating, the first glimpse of the technological revolution that was to make the Viking Age feasible, and the Vikings so

formidable. Here they are, beaked at both ends and powered by oars, but they seem to be overwhelmingly associated with a symbolic rather than an actual voyage, a spirit journey to the Otherworld.

The sun, the axe, the ship, and the phallus: such were the dominant themes of Scandinavian art and religion in the Bronze Age. They complement the vigour and excellence of the Bronze Age craftsmen. It is from this period that archaeology has recovered the superbly cast trumpets or *lurs*, helmets with great curving horns, and small bronze figurines of men wearing horned helmets and holding ceremonial axes (although the axe-arms have since been lost). These helmets are almost certainly the ritual headgear of priests or priest-gods used in magical cult activities, perhaps to invoke the virility and courage of a bull for fertility or battle rites. It was from these finds that the early antiquarians envisaged the Vikings as wearing horned helmets in battle, a popular misconception that dies hard; it would be difficult to imagine a more burdensome and potentially dangerous encumbrance for a warrior in action.

Bronze Age Scandinavia was removed from Viking Age Scandinavia by several centuries, but it is during the Bronze Age that we first begin to recognize some of the characteristics that the rest of the world would later associate with the Vikings—their warrior vigour, their taste for battle, their furious faith in belligerent gods. The Bronze Age Scandinavians were by now distinctly Germanic, sharing an identifiable Germanic culture and religion including divinities whose descendants came to dominate the Norse pantheon as Óðin, Thór and Frey.

Archaeology suggests that the conspicuous wealth of the Bronze Age diminished considerably in the first millennium BC, with the arrival of the Iron Age. The richness and quality of grave goods dwindled. The climate deteriorated sharply, the northern regions of Scandinavia became uninhabitable and there was widespread impoverishment. This was the Scandinavia that Pytheas visited around 330 BC, and his picture is corroborated by the archaeological record. The Iron Age, which began around 500 BC, was a sad period of decline for Scandinavia compared with the Bronze Age.

Historians tend to divide the Scandinavian Iron Age into three distinct phases: the 'Celtic' Iron Age (from 500 BC to *Anno Domini*), the 'Roman' Iron Age (dated *Anno Domini* to AD 400), and the 'Germanic' Iron Age (from AD 400 to the start of the Viking Age around AD 800). During the first phase, while Scandinavia was contracting, it was the turn of the Celtic peoples of central Europe to experience a period of expansion. From their homelands around the Upper Rhine and the Danube basin they began to spill outwards, overrunning western Europe to the coasts of the Atlantic, pressing over into the British Isles, going south into Spain, Italy and Greece, and driving east towards Scythia and Asia Minor. Ruthless and acquisitive, the Celts with their

Above: This memorial picture stone from Martebo in Gotland, dating from the fifth century AD, *is one of the earliest known. The whorls symbolize the sun, decorated with vignettes from the hunt. Picture stones were first used in Gotland as monuments to the dead at the start of the 'Germanic' Iron Age*

Top right: Deity in a horned helmet, from the late Bronze Age, found at Grevens Vaeng in Zealand. Originally he carried an upraised axe in his right hand, and was fastened to a mirror-image twin alongside him by the metal strap at his knees

Right: Late Bronze Age trumpet, or lur, from Denmark. Several of these lurs have been found in peat-bogs, often in pairs, and many are so well preserved that they can still be played, but neither the kind of music produced nor the reason why they were deposited in peat-bogs is known

war-chariots and sophisticated iron weapons were the most dynamic peoples of Europe at the time; an aristocratic warrior society that brooked no opposition. They threw Europe into confusion, as the Germanic tribes were to do in their turn. The traditional trade-routes from the north to the Mediterranean across central Europe were disrupted, and Pytheas' expedition by sea was doubtless intended to find an alternative, safer route to the north that would circumvent the Celtic upheaval and cut out the Celtic middlemen who now controlled the trade-routes.

But the impetus of the Celts never carried them into Scandinavia; and as the Celtic surge waned, the tribes of southern Scandinavia began to stir, spurred on by poverty and hard conditions in their homelands. Two tribes are mentioned by Strabo of Pontus in the first century BC: the Teutones and the Cimbri of Jutland. It is clear that by then it was the turn of the Celts to be on the defensive: 'They say that the Belgae are the bravest. . . . They alone are said to have resisted the attack of the German tribes, the Cimbri and the Teutones.'

The 'Roman' Iron Age brought Scandinavia into the sphere of recorded history for the first time. In AD 5, a Roman fleet made a reconnaissance to Jutland. But the Romans never attempted to conquer Scandinavia; four years after the naval reconnaissance to Jutland, the Romans were soundly defeated by the Teutones, and they probably decided that an attempt to extend their imperial rule into the Scandinavian peninsula was not a sound military proposition. They were to have their hands full soon enough when they faced the Germanic tribes at the Rhine and the Danube. The first ominous mobilizations of the Teutones and the Cimbri were soon followed by the movement of the Lombards, the Burgundians, and the Goths. Scandinavia was about to become what the Gothic historian Jordanes would later call 'the factory of peoples and the matrix of nations'.

During this period, the Scandinavians themselves were not literate, although they would soon be using an alphabet of twig-like characters called 'runes' for inscriptions on weapons and grave-stones. But the classical authorities such as Pliny the Elder, Tacitus and Ptolemy, have left us glimpses of the geography and social organization of Scandinavia at this time. For the first time some of the tribes who were to become the ancestors of the Vikings are mentioned. These include the *Suiones*, for instance, who can be identified with the powerful Svíar (Swedes) of Uppland in eastern Sweden, and the *Goutoi*, who were the Gautar of southern Sweden, and the Geats commemorated in the Anglo-Saxon epic, *Beowulf*.

By the end of the first century AD, Tacitus tells us, the Suiones were the dominant people of Scandinavia, a fierce warrior society in which 'wealth is held in high regard, and that is why they accept one of their number as supreme, with no limit to the ruler's authority and

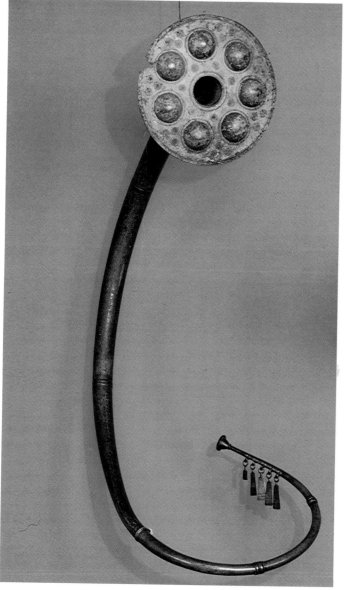

with no mere casual claim to obedience'. The Suiones also had powerful fleets which commanded the Baltic. Once again, the ship arises as a theme, for with the change from Bronze Age to Iron Age there had been a corresponding change in burial customs. The great burial mounds gave way to boat-shaped graves outlined with stones, with taller stones at each end to represent the prow and stern. Symbolic sea-voyages into death: these funeral practices were the forerunners of the genuine ship-burials of the Viking Age.

During the Roman Iron Age the grave-goods became richer again, reflecting a period of increasing prosperity in Scandinavia. As the Celts were subdued by Roman arms, trade started flowing up the Elbe to Jutland and via the Vistula to the Baltic. The Scandinavians developed an eager appetite for southern goods, acquired either through commerce or by force: silks, spices, wines, weapons, brooches, bronze and silver vessels, glass beakers and bowls and fine pottery. In exchange went furs, skins, walrus-ivory, farm-produce and slaves. Rich Scandinavians, both men and women, were laid in their graves surrounded by choice personal possessions imported from the farthest corners of the Roman Empire. Impressive hoards of Roman coins found in Denmark and Sweden show the extent of the trade and the importance attached to bullion. Even the Roman nomenclature for trading terms was incorporated into the Scandinavian language, so that *öre*, the equivalent of *aureus*, came to denote a specific weight and still survives in modern Scandinavian coinage.

The basic economy of Scandinavia remained agricultural, now much strengthened by an improvement in the climate. But it was not a place of pastoral tranquillity. Farms and villages seem to have been in constant danger of raids by cattle-rustlers and slave-traders. Fighting-men abounded, armed with a long-bladed sword, spear, round wooden shield, and bow and arrow. Men had to be robust to survive.

But if times were turbulent in Scandinavia during the Roman Iron Age, it was as nothing compared with the turbulence that was unleashed during the era of the great migrations, as the Roman Empire started collapsing and waves of Germanic tribes surged across Europe. In a welter of bloodshed and movement, Visigoths and Ostrogoths forced their way into Italy and Spain; Franks and Burgundians took Gaul apart; Vandals swung from Andalusia to North Africa; Angles, Saxons and Jutes left Denmark to invade and occupy Britain. It was from this convulsive period that the earliest legends of heroic Norse literature arose, woven round historical figures like Ermanaric the Goth, Attila the Hun, Gundicarius (Gunnar) the Burgundian, and Hygelac of the Geats, whose disastrous raid on the Frisians in AD 521 is recalled in *Beowulf*.

Within Scandinavia itself, there seems to have been perpetual internal strife, centuries of internecine war

Above: The Viking mode of burial has made funeral sites the most valuable sources of information to archaeologists, though not the only ones. This map shows some of the major sites where pre-Viking and Viking artefacts have been found

Right: Stone ship-setting in Blomsholm, near Strömstad in Bohuslän. The position of the grave was marked by the outline of a ship, made up of up-ended stones, with taller stones at each end to represent the stem and stern. Sometimes several graves or cremation pits are found within the one 'ship'. The dead were thought to make a symbolic voyage to the Otherworld

between tribes and chieftains luridly reflected in the legendary histories of those times. Through the haze of semi-mythical stories we begin to discern the figures of divine kings, demigods who were the progenitors of royal houses: Óðin, for instance, was depicted as a war-chief who forced his way from Asia Minor to Jutland, where he left his son Skjöld as ruler, ancestor of the royal Scyldings of Denmark. The Ynglings of Sweden and Norway were thought to descend from a divine tribal chief, Yngvi-Frey.

Archaeology does nothing to clarify the royal history of Scandinavia, but it reinforces the picture of continual warfare. Fortified encampments were built to shelter the villagers while their farms were devastated. Most people who owned treasure prudently buried it—a sure sign of troubled times.

These treasure hoards have been a great boon to archaeologists, for they show that despite the troubled conditions Scandinavia was becoming very rich. Richest of all was Sweden, where the Svíar emerged, as Tacitus had suggested, as the dominant tribe in the areas around modern Stockholm in eastern Sweden. It was now, in the fifth century, as the Roman Iron Age was superseded by the Germanic Iron Age, that the first market towns were founded, starting with Helgö (an island in Lake Mälaren, near Stockholm). Helgö was the first known trading post in Scandinavia of real importance; it is still being excavated, but already enough evidence has emerged to prove that its trading connections were extremely widespread, with goods imported from western Europe and the Mediterranean as well as the Baltic countries. The most remarkable find from Helgö so far is a bronze figure of Buddha, dating from the fifth or sixth century, which had been brought from India.

Europe at this time was being ransacked for treasure and much of it was finding its way back to Scandinavia,

The period of opulence in Scandinavia between AD 400 and 800 is often termed the Age of Gold.
Above left: Decorated bridle mount of gilt-bronze from Gotland, dating from the eighth century. This is one of several mounts by the same artist, using vigorous animal motifs. The composition here is surmounted by an elongated S-shaped animal, its elegant neck terminating in a small head with a large single eye. The whole design is restless and dynamic, surging with the energy of early Viking art.
Above: Silver-plated iron brooch with cloisonné enamel work and mounted with precious stones, from Aker in eastern Norway, in the early Vendel style (seventh century). On the top, two birds face each other with large glass-bead eyes—perhaps they are eagles, or carrion-birds of the battlefield. In the centre-plate there is a large male face with heavy moustaches and staring eyes. Underneath, and upside down, are two animal heads

where it acted as an inspiration for native craftsmen. The centuries of the Germanic Iron Age between AD 400 and 800 were also an Age of Gold, in Sweden at least, a description that is amply justified by the staggering wealth of the aristocratic Swedish cemeteries from this period. It became the custom for chieftains to be buried in huge mounds, sometimes in an actual ship, laden with elaborately ornamented weapons and armour and accompanied by costly personal treasures of gold, bronze, silver and glass.

Wealth of this scale cannot be accounted for simply as the proceeds of looting. The economy of Scandinavia was not only stable, it was expanding. There are indications that at this time both the Norwegians and the Swedes were beginning to move back into the abandoned northern areas where the severe climate of the previous millennium had rendered the land uninhabitable. They were now pressing against their Lapp neighbours (descendants of the original hunter-gatherers) to exploit the vast untapped regions of northern Scandinavia for iron, timber, furs and ivory. Scandinavia was beginning to feel, and enjoy, its strength. While the rest of Europe was racked by invasion and conquest, the Scandinavians were free from the threat of attack from abroad, and could devote their considerable energies to carving out their own kingdoms and creating a vigorous society of their own.

This vigour and self-confidence was particularly apparent in Scandinavian art. It has sometimes been held that the Scandinavians were merely looters, with nothing creative or distinctive to lend to the cultures of the countries they overran, but this is very far from the truth. Scandinavian art during the Age of Gold was the direct forerunner of Viking art, and its major motif was animal ornamentation which fertilized and stimulated other European art-styles—abstract writhing creatures, sinuous gripping beasts, half brutal, half sardonic, always giving an impression of power and originality.

Another developing feature of Scandinavian life during this pre-Viking period, a feature that would play an enormous part in the Viking Age itself, was the Scandinavian boat. Ships had appeared on Bronze Age rock-carvings. Tacitus had described them in the Baltic fleets of the Suiones: 'The shape of their ships differs from the normal in having a prow at both ends, they do not rig sails or fasten their oars in banks at the side.' We have seen that the ship played an increasing part in the funerary and religious rites of the Scandinavians. But they were much more than mere symbols; they were an essential function of the Scandinavian way of life at a time when the sea was the highway of the North. Even the name of Norway simply meant 'North Way' —not so much a country as a sea-route.

No one knows for certain what kind of boats the earliest Scandinavians used. The 'dug-out', or hollowed log, is the most widespread type of primitive craft in the world, but it seems more than probable that the early Scandinavians used 'skin-boats', boats with wooden frameworks over which cured cow-hides were stretched. It has been convincingly argued, and demonstrated by experimental archaeology, that the Bronze Age boats depicted in Norwegian and Swedish rock-carvings can only have been skin-boats. Such boats, it is thought, developed naturally into the plank-built vessels of the early Iron Age.

The earliest boat recovered by archaeology is the Hjortspring boat, dating from about 350 BC, which was excavated from a bog in southern Denmark in 1921. It was a wooden war-canoe capable of carrying 20 oarsmen (or paddlers, for there was no sign of rowlocks), with a large steering oar at each end, so that it could be propelled in either direction. The Hjortspring boat had no sail—the sail was, in fact, a Viking refinement.

The next boat in the archaeological record is the Nydam boat, built nearly seven centuries later and dating from AD 350 to 400. This boat was excavated from a bog in southern Jutland in 1864. It was very large: its oak planks were 82 feet (25 m) long and 20 inches (51 cm) broad, with rowlocks for 30 oars on each side. This was unmistakeably a war vessel, and like the Hjortspring boat it had been deposited in the bog as a votive offering to the gods, an offering of captured war equipment. This was the kind of boat in which the Anglo-Saxons reached England and already the embryonic Viking features are evident even though it was rowed, not sailed. It had the same elegant clinker-built lines as Viking ships, the high stem and stern that Tacitus had remarked upon and the massive steering-paddle on the starboard (steer-board) side. The great Anglo-Saxon warship whose traces were found in a burial mound at Sutton Hoo in England in 1939, which dated from the early seventh century, is a clear descendant of the techniques used in the Nydam boat.

The last significant boat-find from pre-Viking times is the Kvalsund ship, excavated from a bog in western Norway and dating from about AD 700, somewhat later than the Sutton Hoo ship. It, too, was a warship, nearly 60 feet (18 m) long, with a broad hull and no deck of any kind. Like its predecessors, the Kvalsund ship had no trace of a mast or rigging, but the future use of a mast is adumbrated because the Kvalsund ship, unlike the earlier ones, had a rudimentary keel instead of a simple flat bottom plank. With only a bottom plank, the hulls of these light and flexible vessels were not strong enough to take the strain of a mast and sail. The development of a proper keel made the mast possible.

It might seem strange that the Scandinavians did not use sail earlier. The sail had long been established in the Mediterranean, and Tacitus had been duly surprised at the lack of sails in the Baltic shipping. But the Scandinavian sailors were operating for the most part in their own coastal waters, or hugging the European coast, and in those conditions oars were just as effective a means of propulsion and manoeuvring as sails. The archaeological record shows a slow but sure development of sound and seaworthy boats which were fast and light, shallow-draughted and with a low freeboard—the ideal boat for rowing.

In the perspective of history, one can see how the pre-Viking boat evolved steadily towards the point when it was ready for the Viking Age. All the other ingredients for the Viking Age had been maturing concurrently: the martial self-confidence, the taste for adventure and expansion, the loose organization of relatively small units owing allegiance to a personal chieftain, the belief in gods who epitomized warrior-like qualities. The self-reliance and the seamanship were there in rich measure. The omens were propitious. All that was needed to unleash the Vikings on the unsuspecting world was the right kind of ship.

Left: Small bronze figure of a Buddha from northern India. It was brought to Sweden during the Migration Period to the island port of Helgö, in Lake Mälaren, near modern Stockholm, and clearly demonstrates the extent of Scandinavian trading contacts. There is a gold caste mark on the forehead, and the eyes are inlaid with silver

Below: Boat motif on a limestone stele from Häggeby, in Sweden, dating from the fifth or sixth century. The boat, which has no mast, is manned by a crew of fourteen oarsmen. It resembles, though in an exaggerated form, the Nydam boat

the dRagon ships

the gReat age of viking expansion

The general term 'Viking Age' covers that period of dynamic expansion between about AD 800 and 1100 when the Scandinavians erupted on to the European stage in an irresistible surge of energy. In the course of these three centuries the Scandinavians drove their way through Russia to the Black Sea and Constantinople, encircled western Europe to penetrate the Mediterranean, overran and occupied large areas of France, England, Ireland and Scotland, founded new colonies in the Faroes, Iceland and Greenland, and stretched the boundaries of the known world by establishing a brief beachhead on the shores of North America.

It was an extraordinary adventure. Suddenly, it seemed, the northern seas were swarming with lean, low-hulled predators with snarling dragon figureheads, manned by men of reckless courage and invincible ferocity. Everywhere they went they plundered, burned and raped. Holy Church in particular was a target for their insensate violence, and ecclesiastical treasures looted from unsuspecting chapels and monasteries flowed back into Scandinavia in an unending stream:

'In a word, although there were an hundred hard-steeled iron heads on one neck, and an hundred sharp, ready, never-rusting brazen tongues in every head, and an hundred garrulous, loud, unceasing voices from every tongue, they could not recount or narrate or enumerate or tell what all the people of Ireland suffered in common, both men and women, laymen and priests, old and young, noble and ignoble, of hardship and injury and oppression in every house from these ruthless, wrathful, foreign, purely pagan people.'

It was the shrill and outraged gibbering of priests, like the writer of this passage from *The War of the Irish and the Foreigners*, which gave the Vikings their reputation for being bloodthirsty savages. Clerics in holy orders were almost the only people who could write in those days, so not only did they give the Vikings an extremely bad press, they also exaggerated their Satanic nature in order to make moral propaganda: the Viking onslaught was to be seen as a divine retribution for sins, requiring repentance and, no doubt, additional offerings to the church.

Happily, this highly coloured attitude to the Vikings is now changing. Modern scholarship is slowly but surely rehabilitating the Vikings. More stress is now laid on their importance in terms of European politics, commerce, thought, exploration, colonization and art. No one would claim that they were all saints, but it is now apparent that they were by no means quite the sinners they have been made out to be.

It was the Viking ship that made the Viking Age possible. In the first place, it gave the early Vikings the advantage of surprise. After the celebrated raid on Lindisfarne, off the coast of Northumberland, in AD 793, the Northumbrian scholar-priest Alcuin wrote: 'Lo, it is some 350 years that we and our forefathers have inhabited this most lovely land, and never before has such a terror appeared in Britain as we have now suffered from a pagan race, nor was it thought possible that such an inroad from the sea could be made . . .'

Today, the Viking longship with its single mast and square sail is one of the most familiar of vessels in the history of marine architecture due to the dramatic discovery, excavation and restoration of three handsome longships from burial mounds in southern Norway: the Oseberg ship, the Gokstad ship and the Tune ship. All three are now on display in the Viking Ship Museum in Oslo. Of the three, only the Tune ship was not completely restored.

Right: Lindisfarne Priory, target of one of the first recorded Viking raids on England, in 793. The Priory was not abandoned until 875, but the raid struck terror and demonstrated the Viking potential for surprise

Gokstad and Oseberg: without doubt the most famous Viking ships in the world.
Below: The Oseberg ship, a royal barge of the ninth century used for the burial of a Norwegian queen. It contained a wealth of beautifully carved furniture and equipment. The curled tip of the prow is not original, but the rest was extraordinarily well preserved.
Inset: The Gokstad ship was a true Viking longship, long, lean and predatory, manned by sixteen pairs of oars

The Oseberg ship, a richly decorated boat intended for coastal waters, dated from the first half of the ninth century. It was an elegant State barge that in its old age had been used for the burial of a queen, who has tentatively been identified with the redoubtable Queen Ása, grandmother of the first king to unite the whole of Norway under one crown late in the ninth century, King Harald Fine-Hair. She was accompanied to the grave by a young slave-girl, and all the appropriate furniture and equipment for a continuation after death of the kind of royal existence she had been accustomed to: a wooden wagon, sledges, beds, tapestries, looms, casks, cooking utensils, riding harness, shoes, personal possessions, and an ox.

The Gokstad and Tune ships are dated somewhat later in the ninth century. They, too, were clearly associated with royal or high-ranking funerals and it has been suggested that Gokstad was the grave of Olaf, king of Vestfold, who died around 870.

The Gokstad ship, unlike Oseberg, was a true warship: nearly 80 feet (25 m) long, weighing about twenty metric tonnes fully laden but drawing only about three feet (1 m) of water. Like the Oseberg ship, the Gokstad ship had a full keel, but her mast support is considerably stronger—no doubt because the Oseberg ship, which was the earlier, showed signs that her mast construction had proved too weak for all weathers and had had to be repaired. There were holes for 16 pairs of oars which

could be closed by wooden covers on the inside when the boat was sailing, and there was a large steering paddle mounted near the stern on the starboard side.

The Gokstad ship was, and still is, a marvellous example of shipbuilding, representing the culmination of centuries of technological development that stretched in an unbroken line from the Hjortspring boat 1,300 years earlier. It was designed for coastal operations carrying a crew of 35. Its seaworthiness for ocean crossings was demonstrated in 1893 when an exact replica sailed from Norway to Newfoundland during stormy weather in precisely 28 days.

It is clear from all the sources, however, that the Vikings preferred to hug the coast whenever possible. Any cooking had to be done ashore, so that at sea the men would have to make do with dried fish and cold cured meat. There was very little cover on board; the crew slept on deck in double sleeping-bags made of leather. Whenever circumstances allowed, they preferred to make camp on land and spend the night under canvas.

Open-sea navigation tended to be fairly risky too, although there is no general agreement amongst scholars about how sophisticated the Viking navigational techniques actually were. It seems clear that some helmsmen had sufficient knowledge of astronomy to be able to steer along a latitude. They kept position by observing the sun's maximum height at noon and thereby calculating latitude by comparison with other known places. They may also have been armed with a 'sunstone' for overcast days, a translucent piece of Iceland spar which polarized the light and became opaque when turned towards the invisible sun. Certainly by the tenth century they were using notched bearing-dials with which to establish the points of the compass by reference to the sun. For the most part, however, Viking mariners seem to have worked on knowledge of coastlines and practical sailing instructions passed by word of mouth.

It is the Viking longships that have claimed popular attention in the past. But not all Viking ships were warships; in fact the bulk of Viking shipping took the form of cargo-boats, for trade, colonization and deep-sea exploration. Chief amongst them was the *knörr*, a bulky, buxom-breasted tramp-ship that was the real maid-of-all-work of the northern seas.

The only knörr that archaeology has recovered so far was salvaged from the shallow waters of Roskilde Fjord in Denmark in 1962. She had been scuttled in the eleventh century, along with four other Viking ships (two warships, a small Baltic trader, and a ferry-boat) to block the main navigational channel against Norwegian raiders. All five ships are now being restored in the Viking Ship Museum in Roskilde.

The knörr was shorter and stubbier than the warships, built mainly of pine, more than 50 feet (15·5 m) long and 15 feet (4·5 m) wide. She had a half-deck fore and

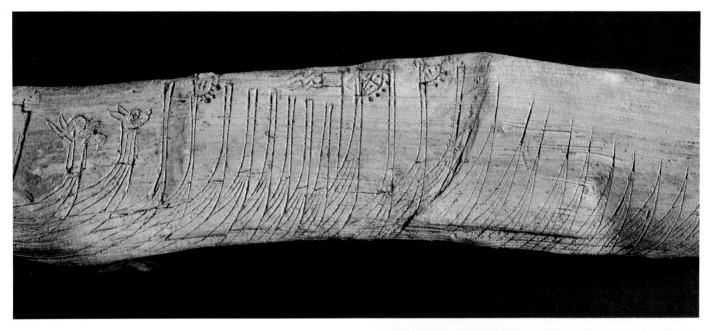

aft, and an open hold amidships for accommodating cargo and provisions for long journeys. She was essentially a sailing-vessel and, unlike the warships, which could be rowed fast for greater manoeuvrability in battle or in close waters, she had only a few oar-holes fore and aft for ponderous manoeuvres in harbour. She was more stoutly built than the warships, which could be beached on a sandy shore during raids and could even be carried overland by the normal ship's complement. The knörr was designed for deep-sea work in all weathers; in the flamboyant diction of the poets she was 'the ocean-striding bison'.

Such then were the ships in which the Vikings embarked on their momentous adventure. But it would be a mistake to think of it as a concerted movement, a conscious attempt at imperialism. Scandinavia itself was anything but united. Different countries, different regions, even different districts had their own allegiances. The term 'Viking Age' is merely a convenience term, as loose and as misleading as 'Dark Ages'.

Even the word *Viking* itself, as a generic term for Scandinavians of this period, is obscure. A number of ingenious derivations have been suggested, but it seems to be related to the Old Norse word *vik*, meaning 'bay' or 'creek', suggesting that it was applied to men who kept their ships in bays and creeks for either warlike or commercial purposes. Soon, however, it came to be exclusively associated with Scandinavians who were raiders and soldiers of fortune.

It is customary to date the start of the Viking Age to around the year 800. In 789, according to the *Anglo-Saxon Chronicle*, there was a brawl on the quayside at Portland, on the Dorset coast of England, between three Norwegian crews and the local authorities, during which the Sheriff of Dorset and his retinue were killed. The raids proper started with the unexpected assault on Lindisfarne that Alcuin had mourned in 793, followed

Top: A Norse fleet, incised on a piece of wood about 7 inches (18 cm) long, found at Bergen and dating from the first half of the thirteenth century. Some of the prows carry dragon-heads or weather-vanes

Above: Bronze-gilt engraved weather-vane from Heggen Church in Norway, probably originally used as a weather-vane or standard on the prow of a ship, as shown on the Bergen carving. The design is in the Ringerike style, with the characteristic long-drawn-out tendrils

Top right: The Viking travels, whether for trade, conquest or settlement, were remarkably extensive. To the West they reached Newfoundland and possibly went farther into North America; to the East they went as traders, exploiting the rivers where possible but reaching Baghdad and the silk routes by land. (Water routes are in blue, land routes in green, and areas of settlement in orange)

Below right: Assorted coins, mostly Byzantine and Islamic, demonstrate the extent of Viking travels

by sporadic raids on another monastery in Northumbria (probably Jarrow) and then Iona and Ireland. But it was not until the 830s that Viking raids on Europe became frequent and co-ordinated.

It is now becoming amply clear that the Scandinavians had been on the move long before this, however: not as 'Vikings' but as traders and settlers. Recent excavations in Shetland and the Orkneys prove that Scandinavian settlers had arrived long before the Viking raids began. They were farmers who quickly absorbed the local population—the Picts—and their culture. The archaeological record suggests a process of peaceful assimilation; the earliest levels of Norse occupation have yielded almost no traces of weapons. The earliest settlers borrowed the existing and sometimes surprisingly sophisticated Pictish customs, household utensils and art-forms, making them their own.

In England, too, the first Scandinavians were almost certainly not raiders. The raid on Lindisfarne may not have come as quite such a bolt from the blue as Alcuin believed (after all, he was living in France at the time as an adviser to the Emperor Charlemagne). Returning to the raid described in the *Anglo-Saxon Chronicle*, it seems that the Sheriff of Dorset had expected the Norwegian newcomers to be merchants rather than potential enemies, and tempers had only flared when the Sheriff somewhat imperiously ordered them to be sent to the royal villa at Dorchester. One can surely assume that there had already been trade contacts between England and Scandinavia, and that this one deserved comment in the *Chronicle* only because it had ended in bloodshed.

Looking east, the same pattern is apparent. The Swedes were busy trading in the Baltic long before the Viking Age began. The smaller of the merchant vessels found in Roskilde Fjord was much more lightly constructed than the knörr, designed for work in coastal waters and rivers, and light enough to be hauled over

land if necessary. Boats like this enabled the Swedes to penetrate Russia in their search for wealth, but they went essentially as traders. They pioneered two major trade-routes down to the Black Sea and the Caspian. One went up the River Volkhov to Novgorod and then overland to the Dnieper and thence all the way to Constantinople; the other was via the Volga, from which they could also reach the silk route from China at a point somewhere near the Aral Sea.

In fact, it was the Swedes who actually created the future Russian state by founding the great cities of European Russia—Novgorod, Kiev, Smolensk—although Russian archaeologists stress the Slavic origins of artefacts found during excavations. The Swedes also seem to have given Russia its name: in 860, according to the *Russian Primary Chronicle*, the people of central European Russia asked a people called the *Rus* to bring order to their country, and it was a Scandinavian called

Rurik who answered the call and founded Novgorod. The precise derivation of the word *Rus* is a matter of argument, but there can be no doubt that the Swedes played a significant, indeed decisive, part in the development of the Russian trading posts. That they were highly successful is amply evidenced by the wealth of goods from all over the East found by archaeologists on the site of the great Swedish market-town of Birka, which flourished from around AD 800 to 950. Apart from silks, spices, furs and metalwork, nearly 60,000 Arabic coins have now been unearthed in Scandinavia — clear indication of the extent of the commerce and the scale of prosperity it engendered.

Trade on this scale had to be protected, of course, and the Swedes were warriors as well as traders. Many of them became mercenaries in Constantinople, where they formed the celebrated Varangian Guard in the service of the emperors. These were not raiders but highly professional troops, a sort of Byzantine Foreign Legion, highly prized not only for their valour but also for their loyalty to their lord.

The Vikings called Russia 'Greater Sweden', but there was never any question of conquest, or annexation. To the Swedes, Russia was a rich and inviting market to exploit. It is quite clear that those Scandinavians who settled there as traders, or who went on to Constantinople, quickly became integrated. They supplied the initial dynamic, the entrepreneurial energy to get towns started, but the towns themselves quickly became essentially Slavic, not Scandinavian.

In Ireland, too, despite the hysterical reactions of the Irish clergy which would suggest the opposite, the Vikings founded the first towns. Vikings must also have taken part in the endless internecine squabbles of the Irish chieftains. Archaeological excavations in the heart of Dublin are year by year revealing the extent of the

Viking city founded there in the middle of the ninth century. Apart from Dublin, the Vikings founded other trading-centres like Limerick, Waterford, Wicklow and Wexford. They injected mercantilism into the simple pastoral economy of Ireland, bringing the Irish into the mainstream of European trade.

Like the Swedes in Russia, the Vikings in Ireland were warriors as well. The Irish Annals are laden with tales of Viking atrocities, but they were written long after the event. The major source, *The War of the Irish with the Foreigners*, which was written in the twelfth century, is little more than an extended panegyric for the Irish King and hero Brian Boru, who fell at the Battle of Clontarf in 1014. It is nationalistic propaganda, inventing for Ireland an image of national resistance against the pagan hordes. It is now established, however, that raiding monasteries was already a favourite Irish pastime long before the Vikings arrived, and although Viking bands played a part in many of the local battles it was usually as mercenaries, rather than as conquerors.

The Vikings were certainly not the invincible iron-men they have become in popular legend. They were usually too loosely organized to be really effective as fighting units, and they were frequently defeated when they faced regular, trained troops. They were at their most successful as hit-and-run 'commandos', making lightning sea-borne strikes against coastal targets and escaping before proper defences could be organized.

Contemporary writers also seem to have exaggerated greatly the numbers of Vikings who were involved in warfare. Even where formal armies were created with openly territorial or imperial ambitions the chroniclers consistently overestimated their size. The 'Great Heathen Horde' which invaded Northumbria in 865 probably numbered little more than 500 men. The Danish invasions of the following century, when the unfortunate King Ethelred the Unready of England bought off Svein Fork-Beard year after year, were no longer Viking in the true sense: these were highly organized expeditions for political and financial gain, manned by professional soldiers and mercenaries who were quartered in great military bases in Denmark. By the tenth century, centralized power in the Scandinavian nations was altering the whole Viking concept; the Scandinavian kings were no longer sea-rovers but men with considerable political muscle, intent on making a large impact on the European stage.

The Viking interest in England illustrates these changes very well. Although King Alfred the Great is remembered as a national hero who drove out the Viking invaders, it should be remembered that in 886 he made a treaty with the Danes which formally recognized the partition of England. The northern part of England became known as the Danelaw and was recognized as a separate and foreign political entity on English soil with its own administrative and legal institutions imported direct from Scandinavia. This became an excellent example of turning swords into ploughshares, for the settlers who quickly proceeded to revitalize the economy and culture of northern England were none other than the 'Great Heathen Horde' who had landed in 865, and now wanted land to settle. The later Danish invasions under Svein Fork-Beard, which led to the short-lived annexation of England under the Danish King Canute, was a strictly imperial venture to capture a throne and create an empire.

That their control of the English throne was short-lived seems somehow typical of the Vikings. It is as if they were natural nomads—nomads of the sea—who tended to lose their distinctive identity when they settled on land. Only one of the countless Vikings who made forays against continental Europe made any lasting impression—a Norwegian freebooter called Ganger-Rolf (apparently called 'Ganger', meaning one who walks, because he was so big that no horse could carry him). In 911 he tried unsuccessfully to besiege Chartres, but later he acquired by treaty from the king of France an extensive corner of northern France. Here, as 'Rollo', he established a permanent Norse presence: so permanent that it became known as Normandy, the land of the Northmen or Normans. The robust energy of the Vikings blended with the local culture to produce a powerful feudal principality which, under Duke William 150 years later, conquered and occupied England with surprising ease.

It was only in the islands to the north of Scotland, where they remained seafarers, that the Vikings retained their natural ethos and culture. The Norse earldom of Shetland and the Orkneys remained distinctively Norse until the thirteenth century, and did not become part of the Kingdom of Scotland until 1468. Even in the twelfth century, when St Magnus Cathedral was being built in Kirkwall, there were individuals in the Orkneys like Svein Ásleifsson who were still living the traditional life of the Viking: farming in spring and autumn, making Viking expeditions in the summer, and feasting with his henchmen all winter long. The building of St Magnus Cathedral, the most impressive and enduring of all Norse monuments in Britain, was both the climax and the end of the Viking Age in the northern islands. It embodied the formal change from a pagan mythology to institutionalized Christianity that had started two centuries earlier. This putting down of massive stone roots also symbolized the final shift from sea to land. Nomads no longer, the Norsemen of the northern islands ceased to be Vikings, and within a short time it was the turn of the Orkney chroniclers to complain bitterly about sea-borne raids—from the Hebrideans!

One has to look even further north, out to the Atlantic, to find the most enduring results of the great Viking expansions: in Iceland, and to a lesser extent in the Faroes. Both were practically empty when the first Norse settlers arrived in the ninth century; the only inhabitants were Irish hermits who had made their way there and who left hastily when the Vikings arrived.

Iceland provided the ideal environment for the creation of a distinctive Norse community, and has remained so to this day. Here the nomads of the sea could settle undisturbed and create a State of their own. The constitution which came most naturally to the Vikings was not a monarchy but a republic, a parliamentary commonwealth. This suited the nature and ethics of men who prided themselves on their independence. In the ideal, or idealized, Viking ship, the leader had only been *primus inter pares*; and this was the concept they took ashore with them in Iceland. And in an oblique way they remained nomads, for in a land without an indigenous source of building timber they insisted on building in timber imported at considerable expense and effort from Norway or even North America. It was

as though they were averse to putting their roots down too strongly. While the Norsemen in the Orkneys and in Greenland built a fine cathedral in stone, the Norsemen of Iceland built their cathedrals of timber. Indeed, the timber cathedral built at Skálholt in the twelfth century was enormous, larger than any stave-church in Scandinavia and capable of seating 700 people. It was only when the Icelanders gradually ceased to be shipowners and came to rely on Norway for their shipping trade that Iceland lost her independence in 1262 to become a Scandinavian colony. It was not until 1944 that she regained her independence as a republic.

Iceland was never a Viking state in the accepted sense of the term. No Viking raids were launched from Iceland, although Icelanders frequently went abroad as young men to win fame and fortune with Viking bands, to serve as court-poets to Scandinavian kings, or even to join the Varangian Guard. But it was Viking in a more

Viking weaponry also acted as showpieces for Viking craftsmanship.
Top left: Sword with a hilt of silver, decorated in the English style, found at Skåne in Sweden.
Top right: Bronze spear with decorated silver hilt, found in Sweden.
Bottom: The great axe from Mammen in Jutland, dating from the tenth century. The design, inlaid with silver wire, depicts a bird-animal with limbs like acanthus plants and spiralling thighs. A Viking's axe had ceremonial as well as battle functions, and was much used for display

essential way: a nation of farmers with a wanderlust, of seamen settled on land, of peasants who liked to behave like princes, of democrats with an aristocratic urge.

The Icelanders have remained Nordic, and retained more of the original Scandinavian features than any other country outside the Scandinavia peninsula. Even the language is still almost unadulterated, the original tongue spoken by the Vikings. By some freak of environment and history, the Icelanders became the repositories of Viking lore, the only Scandinavian nation to write down their history, poetry and mythology in the vernacular. As soon as Iceland was converted to Christianity by parliamentary decree, in the year 1000, a literary tradition began to evolve that culminated in the classical Icelandic sagas of the thirteenth century. These sagas were prose narratives of the history of early Iceland and the Scandinavian kings, composed as formal literary works of learning and entertainment. Concurrently, there was a vigorous tradition of poetry composition. Without exception, all the Scandinavian court-poets were Icelanders, and it was in Iceland that the earliest Germanic heroic and mythological lays were remembered and recorded on calfskin, in the two works known as the Eddas. Between them, the sagas and the Eddas are our richest documentary sources for the Viking Age.

The Viking adventure did not end with Iceland. From Iceland, emigrants sallied forth to settle in Greenland, and from there Viking adventurers braved the unknown perils of the Atlantic to discover and attempt to settle North America, the Vínland of the sagas. But the Vínland exploit did not last long. The colonists, led by the Icelander Thorfinn Karlsefni, arrived early in the eleventh century, but they were too few, their lines of communication with the homeland were too long, and their weapons, albeit of iron, were not destructive enough to keep at bay, far less massacre, the indigenous tribes of Red Indians who resented their incursions. After three years these would-be colonists returned home to Greenland and Iceland. Some anthropologists have discerned in Indian folklore lingering memories of a divine white master-race which they relate to the Viking presence. Despite extravagent effort, archaeologists have so far found only one authenticated Viking site, on Newfoundland. Nevertheless, it seems that for another 300 years, occasional Viking expeditions visited North America to collect timber for treeless Iceland.

The Greenland settlement lasted much longer, but came to a worse end. As the climate deteriorated in the later Middle Ages, Greenland slowly became uninhabitable for Europeans. By the early fifteenth century, the coasts were choked with pack-ice. No ships could reach the beleaguered Norsemen and by the end of the century, when Christopher Columbus was rediscovering the New World, the Norse Greenlanders had vanished from history.

hammer and cross

the coming of the new religion

Above: Bishop's or abbot's bronze crozier or stave, inlaid with enamel, from Helgö in Sweden, dating from the eighth century. This particular piece can hardly be anything other than loot from Ireland, but missionary bishops were busy in Scandinavia from the start of the Viking Age, and Christianity would eventually draw the sting of the Vikings
Left: Face of a Viking—carved figurehead from the cart found in the Oseberg ship. In repose, the face has none of the mindless, fanatical ferocity so often associated with the Vikings by later writers. Strength, determination, and pride—these were the basic traits of the Vikings

By the end of the eleventh century the great Viking impetus had petered out, either through being absorbed or by transforming itself into formal European power-politics. But what caused it in the first place? What were the motives behind this extraordinary surge of expansion? Among the many possible driving forces we could list land-hunger, greed, imperialism, love of adventure, natural aggression, opportunism, bloody-mindedness, or simply wanderlust.

Certainly, there is no single, simple answer, and it could have been any combination of all of these things. It is foolish to attempt to generalize about the Viking Age, for within that portmanteau phrase are packed a hundred inconsistencies. It was not a centralized movement; only sporadically was it directed towards specific ends, like the political determination to conquer England.

One or two contributory factors can be isolated with

some assurance. The principal one seems to be land-pressure. There is evidence that in the seventh century there was a population explosion in Scandinavia which left its mark in a movement into uninhabited areas in the northern valleys in a search for more land. Cause and effect are always hard to disentangle, but it coincided with improvements in metallurgy that made the clearing of virgin forests easier, and with the increasing commercial prosperity of Sweden and, to a lesser extent, Denmark and Norway.

We can easily imagine bustling farming households with several hardy young sons growing up. Only the eldest is going to inherit the farm; the others will have to make their own way. Emigration was one way, and another was lawlessness and piracy in an age when both brought quick returns.

Political pressure, too, certainly played a role. For generations, each valley and district had been largely a

law unto itself, owing loose allegiance to a natural or elected local chieftain. Gradually, more powerful men began to make their presence felt. Footloose young men could be attracted to their service, to take over neighbouring areas by force or the threat of force. Men who had no stomach for subservience, or who fell out with more powerful rivals, might feel it more acceptable or prudent to seek new pastures. The Icelandic sagas tend to emphasize this aspect as an explanation for the motives behind the settlement of Iceland, telling of shiploads of proud freeborn men who resented the attempts by King Harald Fine-Hair to impose his centralized royal authority on the whole of Norway. It is even suggested that King Harald became so alarmed at the wholesale emigration to Iceland that he forbade it, or tried to, which seems slightly contradictory behaviour if the emigrants were, in effect, refugees from his own actions. It is, no doubt, an over-simplified

Above: The wastelands of the far North—an aerial landscape view of Brattahlid in Greenland, the eastern settlement. The Norsemen were inveterate explorers, and would settle in lands that no other Europeans would tackle. Greenland was on the edge of the habitable world for white men, but in sheltered valleys at the roots of the great ice-caps, settlers from Iceland found land fit for farming, and established a colony that lasted for 500 years until the minor ice age of late medieval times

and idealized viewpoint, but it is central to the Icelanders' interpretation of their early history.

Once the movement had started, for whatever reason, the manifest successes of those who took part in it would certainly breed a spirit of emulation. There was land to be had, almost for the asking, to the west over the sea. There were markets that could be spectacularly exploited, to the east. For the strong-arm men, the newly developed Viking sailing-ship made a whole new range of tempting and unsuspecting targets accessible. Politically, too, new opportunities were opening up: Denmark, which was a much more organized state than Norway, had been eyeing the Frankish empire under Charlemagne for a long time, and when Charlemagne died in 814 and the empire started breaking up under his son, the Danes were ready to move in.

As the Scandinavians, both individually and in concert, began to realize their own strength and to revel in their technological mastery of the sea, it is hardly surprising that they should have begun to exercise it. They had spare manpower, spare energy, spare capacity—the perfect recipe for an upsurge of enterprise. Within this large framework of economic, political, sociological and technological circumstances, it is not so hard to see why the Viking movement should have been as varied as it was: why settlers should have sailed with raiders, merchants with warriors, farmers with explorers, poets with pirates.

The causes of the Viking expansion, then, are multiple and complex, but what of the reasons behind the decline in impetus? Why did the Viking Age fade into legend?

The readiness with which the Vikings became absorbed by the indigenous civilizations within which they settled and their capacity to identify with new homelands have already been noted. There was certainly a lack of any highly sophisticated centralizing power, such as the Normans developed, and a lack of coordination between the three major Scandinavian countries—indeed, they were at each other's throats as often as not, thus dissipating the strength that might have made them much more formidable as an imperial force. Ultimately, the Vikings were too individualistic to be organized into an effective machine.

But two other factors should also be considered: the decline of the Viking longship as a fighting instrument against other shipping, and the gradual conversion of the Vikings to Christianity.

The Viking ship as such did not decline during the Viking Age; indeed, it grew better, and bigger. The Gokstad ship of the ninth century had 16 pairs of oars, and until recently it was thought that few Viking warships could have been much bigger. But the Icelandic sagas had spoken of ships that were much longer. Late in the tenth century, King Olaf Tryggvason of Norway was said to have built a ship called the *Long Serpent* which had 34 pairs of oars. And these traditions have now been corroborated by the Roskilde finds, for the larger of the two warships was 90 feet (27 m) long and carried some 25 pairs of oars.

But others could copy the Viking ships, and they did. In 897 King Alfred the Great ordered the building of a navy to deal with the growing number of Viking raiders around the English coasts. The *Anglo-Saxon Chronicle* reported that they were: 'full twice as long as the others; some had 60 oars, and some had more; they were both swifter and steadier and also higher than the others. They were built neither on the Frisian nor on the Danish pattern, but as it seemed to him himself that they would be most efficient.' It could well have been Alfred's navy that spurred the Vikings on to build larger and longer ships, but clearly the Vikings soon lost their overwhelming initial advantage of speed and surprise, and they found themselves at a disadvantage in battle where height above the water could prove conclusive.

Ultimately, it was lack of height that finished the longship as a fighting vessel. The longships had predictably had no success in the Mediterranean against galleys with double or triple banks of oars. In northern waters, too, they lost their advantage against merchant shipping with the development of the two main types of continental cargo-boats, the hulk and the cog. During the late 1960s a medieval cog, the first of its kind to be recovered, was salvaged from the River Weser near Bremen. It was a big, roomy boat, 77 feet (23·5 m) long and 24 feet (7·3 m) high. They were slow and cumbersome, like heavy trucks compared to the racing-car longships, but with their towering sides they were floating fortresses, and in close combat the rowed longships were at a hopeless disadvantage. The Viking shipbuilders tried to even things up by building raised platforms fore and aft, to give their own warriors parity of height, but the cog-builders simply responded by building castles fore and aft themselves. Suddenly, it seemed, the dreaded Viking longship was obsolete, and in the year 1304 the whole Danish navy, comprising a fleet of about 1,100 longships and 40,000 men, was converted to the cog. By then, the lumbering hulk was undisputed mistress of the Hanseatic sea-routes that the Vikings had pioneered.

The effect of Christianity on the Vikings is much harder to chart and evaluate than the effect of the longship's decline. At the outset of the Viking Age, the Scandinavians were to all intents and purposes the only pagan peoples left in Europe. The warlike continental tribes, their Germanic cousins, had all been converted during the migration period. The Anglo-Saxons who settled in England had been converted by St Augustine early in the seventh century. The Saxons on the continent had been forcibly, indeed ferociously, converted by Charlemagne by the end of the eighth century.

The Scandinavian countries resisted formal Christianity for at least two centuries. It was not that they were

anti-Christian: indeed, they were extremely tolerant of other religions (despite the biased accusations hurled at them), and made no attempt to force others to adopt their own polytheistic form of paganism.

The cruel execution by the Danish invaders of King Edmund of East Anglia, and his subsequent sanctification, made a profound impression on the Christian imagination. But there wei special circumstances involved, reputedly a desire for revenge which the sons of Ragnar Hairybreeks nurtured against the English for the death of their father in a snake-pit in York. In general the Vikings, pragmatists that they were, helped themselves to church treasure when it was there, and yet cheerfully submitted to provisional baptism (*prima signatio*) in Christian communities where it was deemed necessary to promote their interests as traders. As the Icelandic *Egil's Saga* puts it: 'This was a common custom of the time, both among merchants and those

Left: Detail from a twelfth-century tapestry from Skog Church, Hälsingland, Sweden, which shows the struggle between Christianity and paganism. Three priests are ringing bells to frighten away evil spirits, represented elsewhere on the tapestry by pagan gods

Right: The magnificently preserved twelfth-century stave church at Fagusnes, Borgund, in Norway. The stave churches are widely believed to be modelled on pagan temples; here, both crosses and dragon-heads were used to protect the church from the powers of darkness—the pagan gods, though banished to the wildest and most deserted areas, were still thought to be a constant menace to the spiritual and temporal welfare of mankind

Below: Statue of Saint Olaf, patron saint of Norway, found in Gotland and dating from the thirteenth century. King Olaf Haraldsson of Norway is credited with the conversion of Norway to Christianity before his martyrdom in 1030 and subsequent canonization

Bottom right: The death of Saint Olaf at the Battle of Stiklestad in 1030. A marginal illumination from the fourteenth-century collection of Icelandic sagas, the Flateyjarbók; it decorates the initial letter of the Saga of Saint Olaf, which was written in the first half of the thirteenth century

Bottom, far right: An earlier royal evangelist, King Olaf Tryggvason who died in the year 1000, failed to convert Norway but was credited with the conversion of several Norse colonies abroad. This marginal illumination from the Saga of Olaf Tryggvason depicts some of his legendary exploits – the killing of a wild boar, and a sea-ogress

mercenaries who joined up with Christians, since those who accepted provisional baptism had full communion with Christians and pagans alike, yet could keep whatever faith was most agreeable to them.' The Danish leader who negotiated the partition of England with King Alfred in 886 accepted baptism as part of the treaty, and although pagan Viking kings struggled for the throne of Northumbria during the following century, the Danelaw south of the Humber settled easily into Christianity.

It was Denmark, with the tide of continental Christianity lapping at its southern borders, that was the first target for Christian evangelism. Charlemagne's son, Louis the Pious, sent the German missionary Anskar to Denmark, and later to Sweden. As a result modest churches were built in the important trading-centres of Hedeby and Ribe in Denmark and Birka in Sweden to cater for the Christian foreigners in residence there as merchants. In the second half of the tenth century, King Harald Blue-Tooth of Denmark was baptised, the Church in Denmark was organized as part of the diocese of Hamburg, and Denmark was set to become an imperial power under Harald's son and grandson, Svein Fork-Beard and Knút (Canute). Harald's father, Gorm the Old, had been a pagan and his mother, Thyri, was a Christian. They were both buried in a great funeral mound at the Danish royal seat at Jelling, but now Harald exhumed their bodies and re-interred them in a small wooden chapel nearby, where he erected the magnificent Jelling memorial stone. This stone was decorated with a figure of Christ, a beast struggling with a snake, and the forthright runic inscription: 'King Harald had this memorial made for Gorm his father and Thyri his mother—the Harald who won for himself all Denmark and Norway, and made the Danes Christian.'

Norway, to whose throne Harald Blue-Tooth had made such sweeping claim, proved more obdurate than

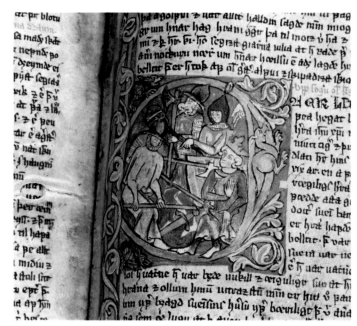

Denmark in the matter of Christianity. Occasional rulers in the tenth century found it politically expedient or spiritually comforting to affect baptism, but it was not until the last decade of the century that a really determined attempt was made to convert the Norwegian population as a whole. This was the avowed intent of King Olaf Tryggvason, who ruled Norway for five turbulent years between 995 and 1000. Olaf was a prototype Viking sea-king. The grandson of Harald Blue-Tooth, he had grown up in Russia, cruised the Baltic as a Viking in his youth, and fought in England with the Danish armies in the 990s. He was converted in England in 994, either by a wise hermit in the Scillies as legend would have it, or in exchange for accepting a vast sum of Danegeld (protection money) from the English.

With money, an army, and a new faith, Olaf Tryggvason's advance to the throne of Norway was irresistible, and he threw himself into the task of spreading the faith with an iron determination that brooked no opposition. According to the later Icelandic historians, he succeeded in converting five countries—Norway, Shetland, the Orkneys, the Faroes, and Iceland. Little is known of the conversion of the northern islands; but King Olaf certainly brought considerable political pressure to bear on Iceland. He sent missionaries and priests, supported the growing Christian party in Iceland against the pagan conservatives, and held the sons of prominent Icelandic pagans as hostages until at a fateful session of the Icelandic Parliament in the summer of the year 1000 the two opposing parties agreed to put their dispute to arbitration and thus avert a threatened civil war and the partition of their country. The arbitrator, himself a pagan, decided in favour of Iceland becoming Christian.

King Olaf's claim to have converted Norway was more exaggerated, and after his death in battle in the year 1000 the country quickly reverted to paganism.

There is disagreement in the sources about the spiritual quality of Olaf Tryggvason's faith, but as a far-travelled man and an ambitious empire-builder he was certainly well aware of the potential political advantages of belonging to the Christian community of Europe and thus keeping behind him the institutionalized strength of the Church.

Another Olaf, Olaf Haraldsson, who was called Olaf the Stout and was later to become Saint Olaf, deserves the decisive credit for converting Norway. He, too, was a footloose Viking with a family claim on the Norwegian throne. He had been baptised while on military service in Normandy, and in 1016 he fought his way to the throne. He proceeded to propagate Christianity in Norway again, by force if necessary. Those who accepted baptism were received into the king's friendship, those who refused were maimed, blinded, or executed. Pagan temples and places of worship were ruthlessly despoiled. At the same time, he built churches throughout Norway and formulated a firm church law regarding their upkeep and administration. In his foreign policy he was less successful, however. He formed an alliance with Sweden against Denmark, but was rather easily defeated by the formidable King Knút and driven into exile. When Olaf tried to make a comeback in 1030 he was defeated in battle and killed, later to be canonized as legends spread of miracles associated with his uncorrupted body.

Sweden was the last of the Viking nations to accept Christianity. Early in the eleventh century a Swedish king had accepted baptism, but few of his people followed his example. It was not until the twelfth century that the great centre of pagan worship at Uppsala was destroyed. Here had stood a temple, according to Adam of Bremen 'entirely decked out with gold', where the people worshipped the gods of their pantheon, and made sinister sacrifices in a nearby

grove. Uppsala was the most celebrated pagan site in Scandinavia, and it is noticeable that only at Uppsala do historians suggest the presence of a vocational priest-hood under the patronage of the king. Elsewhere, paganism was so loosely organized, so lacking in doctrinal or institutional power, that it had no political significance. It can hardly be a coincidence that the only one of the three northern countries with any kind of institutionalized religion should have resisted the on-ward march of Christianity the longest.

It must be asked whether the conversion to Christian-ity made any significant differences either to the Vikings or to the Viking Age. Could its effect have been any-thing other than beneficial? Conventional Christian piety might require a negative answer, but the fact re-mains that the coming of Christianity coincided with the start of the Viking decline in the eleventh century.

Christianity pulled Scandinavia into the intellectual mainstream of medieval Europe, where the Viking nations were unfitted to compete. They did not have the economic resources of their rivals; they had no national institutions, neither socio-political nor re-ligious, to compare with those of the long-established and unified empires of Europe. They were outclassed as national powers, where they had previously been un-matched as freelance opportunists and entrepreneurs.

This might suggest that the Vikings had only flour-ished as takers who had nothing of their own to offer in return. Indeed, that is how they have often been por-trayed: as a race which battened on the achievements of others and gave nothing. But such a view is a travesty.

Apart from their mercantile enterprises, which ex-tended the boundaries of trade to and from unexploited markets, the Vikings have large achievements to their credit which proved of lasting value to Europe. In art, they created a vigorous style which cross-fertilized the art-forms of many other countries: some of the finest ecclesiastical treasures of Ireland, such as the magnificent Shrine of the Crozier of the Abbots of Clonmacnoise, were decorated with the lively and robust patterns of the Ringerike style, imported direct from Scandinavia. Some superb English manuscripts were illuminated with a happy marriage of Ringerike and the sophisti-cated Winchester style during the reign of King Canute. There was nothing crude or derivative about Viking art; the endlessly coiled beasts and tendrils, every inch of space filled with dynamic activity, were a direct and individual expression of virility.

The Norse presence in the British Isles is still reflected in scores of place-names and words. Although the Viking institutions were less sophisticated in some ways than those of the host countries, they had a fundamental democratic quality that was ahead of its time. It was the Vikings, curiously enough, who introduced the word *law* into the English language. They also introduced the principle of juries and majority jury verdicts. They brought with them concepts of justice, albeit rough justice, as well as some comparatively 'liberated' views of the position of women in society, that were still alien to Anglo-Saxon England.

The Vikings extended the boundaries of the known world to the north and west. The Icelanders, who were indefatigable explorers, discovered Spitzbergen some-time before 1170, and Jan Mayen Island in 1194; they discovered and settled Greenland, and explored Baffin Island and North America.

In Iceland itself, the descendants of the original Viking settlers created a vast body of literature that is recog-nized as one of the finest achievements of medieval Europe. That literature enshrines a heroic ethic, a heroic way of life, which has been the envy of succeed-ing generations and which has ultimately overcome the appalling reputation they were given by Christian propagandists.

Left: Hedging your bets—a tenth-century smith's mould for casting both Christian crosses and Thór's hammer. Silver amulets were widely used throughout Scandinavia, and several burials have provided evidence of people wearing both Christian and pagan symbols

Below left: An eleventh-century tombstone from St Paul's Cathedral Churchyard in London. Carved in characteristic Ringerike style, it reflects Viking influence during the reign of King Knút (Canute). The runic inscription reads 'Ginne hath this stone laid, and Toke . . .'

Below: Detail from one face of the massive Jelling Stone, from the Danish Royal Cemetery in Jutland, with a representation of the Crucifixion. The memorial stone was raised in about 985 by the first Christian king of Denmark, King Harald Blue-Tooth, in memory of his parents

the GReat VOID

creation and doom in viking cosmology

In the beginning of time
There was nothing:
Neither sand, nor sea,
Nor cooling surf;
There was no earth,
Nor upper heaven,
No blade of grass—
Only the Great Void.

Völuspá (The Sibyl's Prophecy)

In the beginning there was nothing, only chaos: a chaos of extremes, of violent opposites. The Norsemen called

Left: The monsters of the dark. Detail of a dragon-head on the Mammen horse-collar from Jutland, dating from the tenth century. In the Viking cosmology, the gods were doomed to be destroyed by monsters of the Abyss

it Ginnungagap, the Great Void, the Abyss of Emptiness. But the emptiness was an illusion, a deception, as the Norse word in fact implies. It was not infinite, but finite, charged with overwhelming magic force and pregnant with potential life. The Norsemen did not see creation in terms of a big-bang theory or a steady-state theory; for them, it was a process of predestined evolution, the sparking of life from the cataclysmic fusion of the twin polarities of fire and frost, of light and darkness, and even of good and evil.

It is impossible to give a strictly systematic account of Norse cosmology, for the creation myths do not form a coherent or consistent narrative. There is no 'Authorized Version' to draw upon, and instead we have a number of concepts, sometimes contradictory, that were given expression in mythological lays. At times there is no more than a brief echo of a theme that no longer survives, a solitary allusion to an idea that may

have been the subject of a whole cycle of lays or a cryptic reference buried in a fragment of court-poetry.

An enormous amount of mythological material must have been lost before it was written down, for literature as such only arose in Scandinavia with the advent of Christianity. All that survives was written down long after the event in Iceland where Christianity was fortunately less dogmatic and more tolerant of the pagan past than elsewhere. For two centuries after their conversion, Icelanders cherished the religious traditions of their pagan ancestors and remembered the lays about the old gods and heroes until they were written down in the thirteenth century.

Most of the surviving mythological and heroic lays were gathered together into one major collection of 39 poems, known as the *Elder Edda* or *Poetic Edda*. The manuscript itself, which is called the *Codex Regius*, was written in Iceland around the year 1270 from an original

*Below: The Abyss of Emptiness, the frozen North—
Niflheim. The authors of the Norse cosmology knew all
about the terrors of the northern ice—'Netherwards and
northwards lies the way to Hel.' For them, the searing
heat of the Christian Hell was the lesser of two evils, and
the real enemy was the cold that froze the sinews and
paralysed the will*

compilation (now lost) that is thought to have been
made around 1225. The lays themselves, however, are
very much older; the heroic lays, which are discussed
in the last chapter of this book, have their roots deep in
the pre-Viking world of Germanic legend. All the
linguistic and literary evidence indicates that much of
the poetry, heroic and mythological alike, was already
very ancient by the time it was written down in the
thirteenth century, and that some of it was earlier even
than the settlement of Iceland in the ninth century. The
mythological lays, of which there are ten in the *Elder
Edda*, were not songs of praise to the gods. Some of them
were didactic in purpose, treatises on pagan beliefs and
lore cast in the form of dramatic dialogues between gods
and giants about the creation and doom of the world.
Other lays tell narrative stories about the gods and their
adventures, stories which emphasize the human (and
often humorous) aspects of the gods.

The most potent of all the mythological poems is the *Völuspá* (*The Sibyl's Prophecy*), which was composed in Iceland very late in the pagan period, perhaps even after the formal conversion to Christianity. In the poem, a Sibyl tells Óðin the fate of the gods.

The only attempt to provide a connected and systematic account of Norse cosmology was also made in Iceland in the thirteenth century, in the so-called *Prose Edda* (to distinguish it from the *Elder* or *Poetic Edda*), which was written about the year 1220 by the great Icelandic historian and scholar, Snorri Sturluson. Snorri's Edda is in effect a handbook for poets, designed to teach the traditional techniques of the ancients and explain the pagan literary allusions to be found in their poetry. The mythological material is contained in a long didactic prose narrative, studded with old poetry, called *Gylfaginning* (*The Beguiling of Gylfi*). For the narrative, Snorri used a literary device employed in some of the original mythological lays. The story tells of a legendary Swedish king Gylfi, who travels in disguise to the citadel of the gods and questions the All-Father, Óðin (in the form of a trinity of High, Equally High, and Third) about the beginning of the world and the fate of gods and men. Snorri's sources, for the main part, were the mythological lays, many of which were preserved in the *Elder Edda* as we know it, but some of his source material has not survived anywhere else in the same form. It is important to remember, however, that Snorri's purpose was to help readers understand the early poetry and its myths; his interest in the myths was essentially antiquarian, and however conscientious a scholar he was, he can hardly have failed to rationalize the myths in places, as befitted an erudite Christian intellectual. Today, we too have to conflate the various sources, just as Snorri Sturluson did, to clarify the outlines of Norse cosmology.

It seems that Ginnungagap, the Great Void, consisted of two starkly contrasting regions: a region of dark and freezing fog to the north called Niflheim (later to be known as the realm of death), and a region of fire and flame to the south called Múspell (which became the home of the future destroyers of the world, presided over by the Fire Giant Surt, after whom the new volcanic island of Surtsey was named). The eleven rivers of Niflheim froze, and layers of congealed fog rose up to spread over everything in Ginnungagap: 'And Ginnungagap, which lay to the north, was filled with a crushing weight of ice and frost, with gusting rain within; while the southern region of Ginnungagap glared with sparks and embers that erupted out of Múspell'. When the fiery heat of the south met the frozen wastes of the north, the poison ice of Niflheim melted, and the drops fused into the shape of the first living creature, a terrible giant called Ýmir, ancestor of all the evil race of giants. Ýmir was a hermaphrodite; when he sweated in his sleep, a male and a female grew from his left arm-pit (the ancestors of mankind, according to this version), and with one leg he engendered a six-headed son upon the other—the progenitor of the Frost Giants.

Ýmir received nourishment from another creature shaped from the melting ice, a cow called Auðumbla whose udders spurted four rivers of milk to sustain the giant. To feed herself, the cow licked at the salty blocks of ice: 'When she licked them on the first day, there appeared out of them by evening the hair of a man; the second day, a man's head; and on the third day, a man complete.' This was Búri, the ancestor of the gods.

The stage was now set for the creation of the world. Búri (the name simply means 'Born') had a son who married a giantess, and their offspring were the first three gods: Óðin and his two brothers. These three fell out with the old giant, Ýmir, and killed him. They carried his body to the middle of Ginnungagap, where they fashioned the world from it. From his flesh they made the soil, from his bones they made the mountains, and from his blood they made the seas and the lakes. His toes and teeth they made into rocks and screes, while his hair formed the vegetation. From the dome of his skull they fashioned the sky, and they threw his brains to the winds to form the clouds.

The sky was held up at its four corners by four dwarves called North, South, East and West. These dwarves were maggots who had bred inside Ýmir's carcass and were now given human form and intelligence by the gods, although they continued to inhabit the hills and rocks after the world had been created. They were a lowly race, cunning and treacherous by nature, hostile to gods and mortals alike, but superb craftsmen whose artefacts were much sought after.

To complete the cosmos, the glowing sparks and cinders that gushed out of Múspell were transformed into stars and heavenly bodies, whose movements were ordered by the gods. 'From this labour came the tally of nights and days, and the measuring of the years.' In another tradition recorded by Snorri, the gods gave a giantess called Night and her son Day each a chariot and horses and sent them up to the heavens to drive round the earth once every twenty-four hours: 'Night went first with the horse known as Hrímfaxi [Frosty-Mane] who sprinkles the earth with dew from his bit each morning; Day's horse, Skínfaxi [Shining-Mane], illuminates all the earth and sky with the radiance from his hair.' In yet another myth, two fair children, Sun and Moon, race across the sky because they are each pursued by a wolf—and will eventually be caught and swallowed.

The concept of a bisexual primeval giant who is slain to create the world is familiar from other mythologies. Zeus and his brothers overthrew Cronus. But the myth of Ýmir has its roots deep in Germanic prehistory,

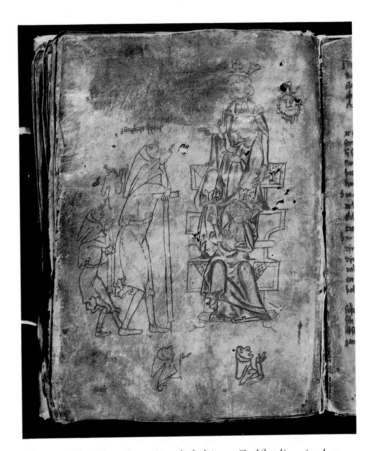

Above: The legendary Swedish king, Gylfi, disguised as 'Gangleri' ('the weary walker') questions Óðin in his triune form as High, Equally High, and Third, about the origins of the world. From a fourteenth-century manuscript of Snorri Sturluson's Prose Edda
Left: Gilded bronze disc representing the sun, from a horse-drawn sun-chariot found in a peat-bog at Trundholm in Zealand, dating from the Early Bronze Age, around 1000 BC. According to Snorri Sturluson, the sun was driven across the skies by Day in a horse-drawn chariot

according to Tacitus: 'In their ancient ballads (their only forms of recorded history), they celebrate Tvisto, a god sprung from the earth, and they assign to him a son called Mannus, the founder of their race.' Similarly, the theme of the primeval life-giving cow can be paralleled by the Egyptian sky-goddess Hathor.

'But where did the men come from who peopled the world?' asked the inquisitive Gylfi in *Gylfaginning*. (He had clearly never heard of Ýmir's fecund armpits, and he is now given an alternative version.) According to Snorri, this was the other great work accomplished by Óðin and his two brothers. Strolling along the seashore one day they came across two logs of driftwood, picked them up, and whittled them into the shape of mankind. The first god, Óðin, gave them life and soul (or spirit); the second gave them understanding and the power of feeling; and the third gave them speech, hearing and sight.

After the creation of mankind, the gods gave them a place to live. The earth was envisaged as being on a flat disc, girt by a mighty ocean (like the *Okeanos* of Greek myth). On the farther shores of this ocean the gods gave a grant of land called Jötunheim to the giants. At the centre of the world disc they established a stronghold for mankind called Miðgarð (Middle Enclosure) which was fortified against the giants by a palisade made from Ýmir's eyebrows. Finally, the gods built their own fastness called Ásgarð (the Enclosure of the Gods), a high citadel on a crag running up from the centre of Miðgarð, fortified by a great wall and connected to earth by the rainbow-bridge, Bifröst. Ásgarð was a beautiful place, resplendent with halls and golden palaces—the Mount Olympus of the North.

The picture of the world that emerges is that of a disc with concentric bands: in the centre was Ásgarð for the gods, then Miðgarð for mankind, then Ocean, and on

Left: Yggdrasil, the World Tree, with a stag browsing on its foliage, from the sculpture on the north wall of the nave of the church at Urnes, in Sogn, Norway. But in its turn, the stag seems to be under attack from the serpent Níðhögg, which bites its throat. At the roots of the great Tree of Life there was a constant struggle between life and death, and the state of the tree reflected the state of the world
Below: North, South, East and West—the four dwarfs who held up the sky at its four corners. This detail of a Viking Age hogback tomb from Haysham, in Lancashire, England, shows two of the dwarfs struggling with their burden

the outside Jötunheim, the home of the giants. But although it was conceived as being flat, it also had three levels: Ásgarð at the top, Miðgarð in the middle, and underneath it, Niflheim, the realm of the dead.

All these realms were held together by Yggdrasil, the World Tree. This was 'the greatest and best of all trees', a mighty ash-tree which was the holy of holies of the gods. Here the gods sat in council every day. This was the centre of the universe: its branches reached the sky and spread over the earth, its three roots stretched into all the realms. At its base lay the Spring or Well of Fate, the source of all wisdom, tended by the three Norns (equivalent to the Fates) who decided the destiny of all living creatures. An eagle perched in its topmost branches; its roots were gnawed by the serpent Níðhögg, with whom the eagle was at war (a squirrel, Ratatosk, ran up and down the tree, sowing mischief between the two), and four stags browsed on its foliage and bark.

Yggdrasil held the fabric of the universe together, a living and sentient being. But it was already under terrible strain: 'The ash Yggdrasil suffers harms, more than men can imagine.' Its trunk was rotting and it suffered fearful torments, even though the Norns kept sprinkling it with healing water from the Spring of Fate. Yggdrasil reflected the parlous condition of the world—a world that was flawed and doomed from the very start.

It is in keeping with the fatalism of the Norse psyche that the world should be doomed from the outset. The seeds of destruction were sown during the creation itself. This doom was summed up in the concept of Ragnarök, the Doom of the Gods. In some corrupt sources, the word was mispelled as *Ragnarökkr*, meaning 'Twilight of the Gods'—an utter misinterpretation.

In *The Sibyl's Prophecy* and other sources, Ragnarök is always visualized in terms of the gods. In the dawn of time, they seemed gay and innocent, but Óðin's mother had been a giantess, and their blood was flawed with latent corruption. The universe they created was always a precarious, vulnerable place, beset by terrible forces of destruction that had constantly to be kept at bay. The demigod Loki, catalyst of evil in the world of the gods, had spawned fearsome monsters whose menace always shadowed the future: Miðgarðsorm (the World Serpent) which lurked in the depths of Ocean, and the baleful wolf Fenrir which lay bound in a cavern in the Otherworld. Across Ocean, the giants of Jötunheim were an ever-present threat to the authority of the gods and the good order of the world. Above all, there was implacable Fate against which even gods were powerless.

The gods were not blameless either. They lied and schemed and cheated. They fought amongst themselves during a dim and distant war between two divine tribes, the Æsir and the Vanir, which ended in an uneasy truce. But the walls of Ásgarð had been shattered by the war, and when the gods employed a skilled smith descended from the giants to rebuild them, they murdered him rather than have to pay the agreed price.

The Sibyl's Prophecy is the only mythological source that sees Ragnarok as the outcome of the depravity of the gods. The poet, no doubt influenced by Christian thinking, passes a moral judgement on the gods; he assembles fragments of myths about the youth of the gods into a sequence of events, a cosmic narrative of innocence and fall, in which Ragnarök is the inevitable consequence of corruption. The other sources, less sophisticated and less systematic, see Ragnarök simply as destiny, remorseless and fore-ordained: in other words, as Doomsday. Óðin the All-Father seeks occult knowledge of the future knowing that there is nevertheless nothing he can do to alter it or avert the impending doom, however much he may try to manipulate events.

The climax is ushered in by the death of Óðin's favourite son, the shining god Baldur, killed by Loki's

treachery. Óðin descends into the Otherworld to force the truth about the future from an ancient and long-dead sibyl, but gets no comfort from it. Throughout the universe, all order is breaking down, dishonesty and treachery abound, fratricide and incest reign unchecked:

> Brothers will battle
> And kill each other,
> Sister's kin
> Commit foul acts.
> There's woe in the world,
> Lechery rampant;
> An axe-age, a sword-age,
> Shields are sundered;
> A storm-age, a wolf-age,
> Before the world crumbles.
> No mercy or quarter
> Will man give to man.

Now a terrible winter sets in called the Fimbul winter. It is the length of three winters with no summer between. Blizzards rage, the frost is like iron, snow sweeps in from every direction. The wolf that was pursuing the sun catches her and swallows her; the moon is likewise caught and the stars are quenched in the heavens. Earthquakes rack the world, mountains crash, and all the fetters that kept the forces of evil at bay are snapped. The dwarves whimper before the doors of their rock-dwellings.

The wolf, Fenrir, breaks free from his prison and advances with gaping jaws that stretch from heaven to earth. The World Serpent writhes in fury and the sea surges over the land. The dead burst from the Other-world and cross the moat of Ocean in the boat called Naglfari, made from dead men's nails. The World Serpent emerges from the depths of Ocean, spewing poison. The heavens are rent asunder, and the Fire

Giants of Múspell come riding forth from the south, led by Surt in a ring of flames, his sword blazing brighter than the sun. The rainbow-bridge, Bifröst, breaks beneath the weight of this mighty host, and now all the adversaries of the gods range themselves for battle on a nearby plain: Fire Giants and Frost Giants, the battalions of the dead, the monsters of land and sea.

Now the watchman of the gods, Heimdall, stands up and blows piercing blasts on his horn to rouse the gods to battle. Óðin goes once more to the Well of Fate for counsel. Yggdrasil, the World Tree, shudders and groans, and heaven and earth are filled with dread.

The gods now arm themselves and sally forth. Óðin rides at the head of his *élite* army of fallen heroes. He and Thór lead the attack on the monstrous offspring of Loki, while Frey makes for Surt and Heimdall for Loki.

The battle that ensues is a scene of epic horror and slaughter. Thór does battle with the World Serpent and eventually kills it, but before he can take nine steps he falls dead to the ground, overcome by its venom. Heimdall and Loki kill each other. Frey and Surt battle it out, but Surt wins in the end and Frey falls dead. The wolf Fenrir, with fire flashing from his eyes and nostrils, devours Óðin, only to have his jaws wrenched apart by Óðin's avenging son.

All the old gods die in that battle. The world shatters and bursts into flame, seared by Surt. The earth sinks into the sea, in a welter of fire and smoke and hissing steam.

But this stupendous cataclysm is not, after all, the end of everything. It is a cyclical ordeal of purification, to which gods as well as mortals are subject. But the World Tree itself does not fall, and in its branches cower two human survivors, a man and a woman who will re-populate the earth when it rises again from the sea, green with grass and fertile. The daughter of the old sun, more radiant than her mother, takes her place in the sky. And though the old gods had perished, their children had not, and two sons of Óðin and two sons of Thór survive to rebuild the home of the gods, Ásgarð:

> She sees arise
> A second time
> Earth from the sea,
> Green with growth.
> Falls cascade,
> The eagle flies high,
> The one from the mountains
> Who stoops for fish. . . .
>
> And there once again,
> Rare and wonderful,
> Golden chessmen
> Will be found on the grass,
> Which the gods had owned
> In olden times.

Above: Óðin at Ragnarök, about to be devoured by his arch-enemy, the wolf Fenrir. Panel from a cross from Andreas, Isle of Man. Óðin, with his raven perched on his shoulder, tries to stab downwards with his spear as the wolf bites at his leg
Left: One of the great enemies of the gods—the World Serpent. A snake-formed brooch from Öland in Sweden, dating from the seventh century. Coiled in upon itself, lurking at the bottom of the Ocean that surrounded Middle Earth, the World Serpent lurks until it bursts forth from the depths at Ragnarök, spewing poison

And now a new Golden Age is at hand: the shining god, Baldur, returns from the Otherworld, and there is a new race of gods who can play once again with their golden chessmen:

> She sees a hall
> More fair than the sun,
> Thatched with gold,
> At Gimlé.
> There shall the gods
> In innocence dwell,
> And live for ever
> A life of bliss.
>
> Then shall the Mighty One
> Come to his kingdom,
> The strong from above,
> Who rules over all.

It is a spell-binding vision, this terrible glimpse of Doomsday and its golden hope for the future. *The Sibyl's Prophecy* is the only one of the sources to offer this strongly Christian image of a better life hereafter: in the other sources, Ragnarök is the end of everything. But even in *The Sibyl's Prophecy* there is still an intimation of a new cycle of doom and destruction on the way, because the last image in the poem is of a dark, glittering dragon swooping down with corpses in the plumage of its wings.

Throughout this cosmic cataclysm with its searing images of terror and destruction, there are constant familiar echoes of universal themes. The figure of Baldur, the innocent victim who must go to the Otherworld, can be paralleled in many mythologies. So, too, can the concept of the world being swallowed up in the sea, and of a universal holocaust. Annihilation is the gloomy stock-in-trade of much religious prophecy.

Norse cosmology is the only one that comes to mind, however, which specifically commits its own particular pantheon to destruction. It may have been coloured by the apprehension of Christianity, but it may also have something to do with the essentially nihilistic ethos of the early Germanic tribes. The Viking world, for all its self-reliance and rumbustious vigour, had a certain innate rootlessness at its core. The concept of eternity was alien to them. Their attitudes to death were informed by a fatalism that stretched beyond the grave: not towards an after-life of everlasting bliss or damnation, but to an even sterner struggle ahead, a struggle that they knew they could not win, a battle from which none would flee and which none would survive. That they were prepared to live with this uncompromising fatalism, and give it such vivid and unambiguous expression, is the ultimate measure of the character of the Vikings.

The monsters of Ragnarök.
Left: Dragon-head from a horse-collar found in Denmark and dating from the tenth century.
Above, left: Animal head-post from the Oseberg ship—an extraordinary baroque composition, the dragon's head and neck are covered with an uninterrupted pattern of gripping-beasts clasping and biting one another.
Right: The gaping jaws of the monster depicted on one of the sledges found in the Oseberg ship.
Against enemies like these, even the gods themselves were ultimately powerless

óðin: the all-father

lord of the gallows and lord of the slain

The Norsemen called their gods the Æsir (the plural form of the word *áss*, meaning 'god'), and their religion was called Ásatrú (belief in the Æsir). These divinities formed a loosely organized unsystematic pantheon of deities and demigods that catered for the varying tastes, needs and social traditions of the Norsemen who worshipped them. Most of them were fundamentally warrior-gods, reflecting the Viking ethos of hardy self-reliance and tough success in everything to which they put their hand, whether it was the adventurer's sword,

Left: The Norse trinity—Óðin, Thór, and Frey. Detail of the woven tapestry from Skog Church, Hälsingland, in Sweden, dating from the twelfth century. On the left, one-eyed Óðin carrying an axe, with a representation of the tree from which he hung; in the centre, Thór, carrying his symbolic hammer in his right hand; and on the right, the fertility god Frey, holding an ear of corn

the farmer's plough, the seaman's rudder, the merchant's scales, or the pioneer's axe. But there were also deities who were essentially fertility gods and goddesses embodying concepts of growth and natural increase, of life and death, that were much older and more primitive than Viking society.

The distinction between these types of deities is reflected by the mythology itself and by the way in which the mythology was rationalized by men like Snorri Sturluson. The Æsir were a particular race of gods who had originally come from Ásaland (Asia), where their chief city had been Ásgarð. Their neighbours there had been another race of demigods, the Vanir, who were fertility gods. In primeval times there had been a war between the Æsir and the Vanir; it had been a bitter and inconclusive struggle, during which the walls of Ásgarð had been shattered, but neither side could win the outright victory. In the end the two tribes of gods made peace and exchanged hostages, and thus it was that a fertility god like Frey came to join the warrior-gods like Óðin and Thór in the pantheon of the Æsir in Ásgarð.

Snorri Sturluson, as befitted a Christian scholar, demoted the pagan gods into ancient war-chiefs in order to provide a harmless framework within which he could tell their stories without affront to the Church. His sources told him that the royal families of Scandinavia traced their descent from these gods: the Ynglings of Sweden looked back to Yngvi-Frey, prototype of divine fertility-kings, whose reign was one of fruitful harvests and peace, while the Norwegians and Danes harked back to more warlike divine ancestors like Skjöld (Shield), the son of Óðin, as the ancestor of the Scyldings. Modern scholars tend to interpret these myths as a folk-memory of a struggle between tribes who worshipped different kinds of gods: a war that ended not in the annihilation of one society, but in the cultural assimilation of the two.

Óðin, Thór and Frey were the foremost of the gods in the Norse pantheon by the time the Viking Age dawned—although not as a trinity, and not necessarily in that order. In the literary sources, and especially in Snorri Sturluson, the paramount god was Óðin: 'Óðin is the highest and oldest of the gods. He governs all things, and however mighty the other gods may be, they all obey him as children do their father. . . . Óðin is called All-Father because he is the father of all the gods.' (Gylfaginning.)

As a statement of fact, this is clearly oversimplified and misleading. There is evidence that the worship of Óðin was a more specialized practice than the widespread veneration of Thór and Frey. And it is also quite clear, from studies of the evolution of Norse mythology from its Germanic origins, that Óðin was by no means the oldest of the gods. He was, if anything, a relative newcomer.

The rock-carvings of the Scandinavian Bronze Age offer the first glimpses of religious concepts in ancient times. Many of these stark scenes appear to be impressions of religious rites. The cults were predominantly masculine, but a number of small bronze, female figurines have also been recovered, which could well represent an earth or fertility goddess. There is one, in particular, who is squeezing the nipple of her right breast; her staring eyes are of gold, and from her position she seems to have been driving a chariot or wagon. Some of the rock-carvings seem to depict a marriage of sky-deities: male and female figures representing the sun or other heavenly bodies are depicted as a nuptial pair, guarded or perhaps blessed by a figure with an upraised axe.

The dominant figure of these carvings is a huge figure with penis erect, brandishing either a spear or an axe: the sky-god. But who was this sky-god? The earliest

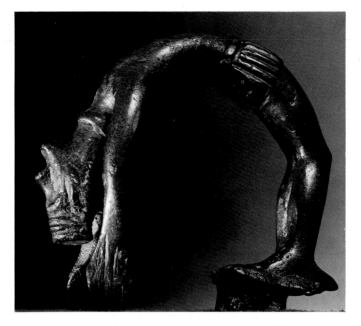

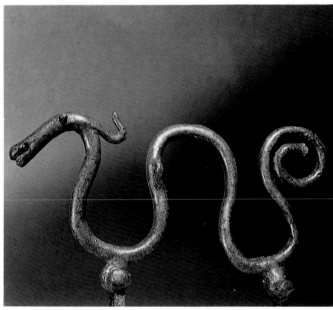

written reference to Germanic religion was made by Caesar in his *De Bello Gallico* in the middle of the first century BC. He was writing about the Germans on the Rhine, and noted that the Germans, unlike the Gauls, had no Druids and no interest in sacrifice; furthermore, they worshipped only such gods as they could see and apprehend, such as the Sun, the Moon, and Vulcan (fire), and knew no other gods even by name. This somewhat threadbare reference is dismissed by scholars, because Caesar's knowledge of the Germans was minimal.

Much more to the point is the *Germania* of Tacitus, written 150 years later, which drew upon eye-witness accounts and earlier written sources that are now lost. Tacitus described in great detail the worship of an Earth Goddess, or *Terra Mater*, called Nerthus, who later appears in Norse mythology (having changed sex) as Njörð, the father of Frey. But Tacitus also mentions two war-gods, Mercury and Mars, who were identified in

The fertility cults of the Scandinavian Bronze Age evidently made use of small bronze figurines.
Far left: Tiny fertility goddess in bronze, measuring just over 2½ inches (6 cm), found at Faardal in Jutland, and dating from the Middle or Late Bronze Age. Her upraised right hand suggests that she is driving a chariot or cart of some kind. Also in the Faardal hoard were several animal heads and a bronze serpent (above, bottom left), which may have formed part of her equipage.
Above, top left: Young girl bending in a backward somersault. The short woollen skirt she wears is paralleled in the garments that have been preserved in the bogs of Jutland.
Above: Woman holding a bowl—bronze decoration on a knife handle, from Itzehoe, Denmark, also dating from the Late Bronze Age

other Roman sources with Óðin and a god called Týr.

There can be little doubt that Týr was originally the sky-god. He was known as Tiwaz in Germany, Tiw in Anglo-Saxon England, and his name has been etymologically equated with what became the Latin *deus* and the Greek Zeus—the original Indo-European All-Father. The evidence of place-names suggests that his cult was strongest in Denmark. The classical authors hinted that prisoners of war were sacrificed to him, and that some tribes regarded him as the highest of the gods. The Romans equated him with their own god of war, Mars, and both are still commemorated in English and French in the name of the third day of the week: Tuesday (*Týsdagur*) and *Mardi* (*dies Martis*).

By the time of the Viking Age, however, Týr had long since lost his ancient pre-eminence as All-Father in the Norse pantheon, and had been relegated to a relatively minor place in the hierarchy. Snorri Sturluson called him a son of Óðin, but echoes of his former omnipotence still remained, for his name was still used by the poets as a synonym for 'god'. For example, a collective name for the gods was the plural form *tívar*, and Óðin himself, in one of his many nicknames, was known as Hánga-týr—God of the Gallows.

Snorri Sturluson described him thus in *Gylfaginning*: 'There is another god, called Týr. He is extremely daring and courageous, and has much say in the outcome of battles, and bold men are well advised to invoke his name.'

The outstanding example of his courage was the part he played in the binding of the wolf Fenrir, in the later creation myths. Fenrir, who was one of the monstrous offspring of Loki and was destined to devour Óðin at Ragnorök, grew up with the gods in Ásgarð. He became so huge and ferocious, however, that none of the gods except Týr dared feed him. The gods had a premonition of the catastrophe this terrible creature would cause, and resolved to chain him so securely that he could never break free. Twice the gods approached him with fetters and playfully challenged him to try his growing strength by seeing if he could break them, and twice, to their dismay, he snapped them with ease. The gods now feared they would never be able to bind him. But a third chain was fashioned for them by the dwarves, those supreme craftsmen of Norse myth. This was a magic bond made from all the secret, invisible and arcane things of the world: the noise of a cat, the beard of a woman, the roots of a mountain, the sinews of a bear, the breath of a fish and the spittle of a bird. It was as smooth and soft as a silken cord and the wolf naturally suspected a trap when the gods approached him with it. Eventually he was persuaded to let himself be bound with it, but only on condition that one of the gods place his own hand in his jaws as a pledge of good faith. The gods were much taken aback, but eventually Týr volunteered to be the hostage and put his right hand in

the wolf's maw. The wolf now consented to have the magic cord wrapped around him, only to find that the more he strained and struggled to break free, the tighter the fetters became. In his rage he bit off Týr's hand, but Fenrir was bound at last, and could be imprisoned in a cavern deep in the Otherworld, there to stay until the cataclysm of Ragnarök. Meanwhile Týr became known in poetry as 'the one-handed god', and would meet his own death at Ragnarök in mortal combat with another fearsome wolf, Garm, who guarded the route to the Otherworld.

Óðin, the god who superseded Týr as All-Father in the Viking pantheon, was an infinitely more complex deity. His name is usually associated with the Old Icelandic adjective *óður*, meaning 'furious, vehement, mad', and Adam of Bremen, writing in the eleventh century, echoes this etymology with the phrase *Wodan, id est furor*—'Wodan, that means fury'. His name

Above left: The huge phallic figure of the sky-god brandishing his spear over the battlefield is the dominating image in this Bronze Age rock carving from Bohuslän, Sweden

Left: Týr, the original sky-god of the Germanic tribes, from a die used for making helmet plates found at Torslunda, on the Baltic island of Öland, and dating from the sixth century AD. It is one of a series of man-and-animal dies, and used to be called 'the Daniel in the Lion's Den motif', but the chained animal is much more suggestive of the wolf Fenrir, whom Týr fettered at the cost of his own hand

Above: The new sky-god, Óðin, is represented by this bronze figurine from Linby, Skåne, in Sweden, dating from the Viking Age

(Germanic *Wotan*, Anglo-Saxon *Woden*) is commemorated in English in the week-day Wednesday, just as his Roman counterpart, Mercury, is commemorated in French in *Mercredi*.

But amongst the pagan poets of Iceland and Norway, Óðin had a host of other names—about 170 in all; some of them reflect his dark and many-sided personality, like 'Evil-Doer', 'Lord of the Gallows', 'Father of Victory', 'Wanderer', 'The Hooded One', 'The One-Eyed', 'All-Knowing', 'Lord of the Slain', and 'All-Father'. Óðin was essentially the *Viking* god: the god of battle, the god of guile, the god of death.

In the extravagant and Christianized encomium in *Gylfaginning*: '[Óðin] lives throughout all ages, ruling his kingdom absolutely and governing all things great and small. He fashioned heaven and earth and the skies and everything that is in them . . . But the greatest is this, that he created Man and gave him immortal spirit which shall never perish though the body crumble to dust or burn to ashes.' This intensely intellectual, literary concept reflects the special place held by Óðin as the patron god of poetry. With his profundity and contradictions and complexity, Óðin appealed to poets more than any other god, and this helps to explain his pre-eminence in the pantheon.

Óðin seems to have become one of the chief gods of the Germanic warrior tribes during or before the early Christian era. In Anglo-Saxon England, Woden was venerated as the ancestor of chieftains and as the supreme god. Hengist and Horsa, the legendary founders of the English nation, were said to be descended from him, as were nearly all the provincial kings according to the Venerable Bede. A handful of English place-names still commemorate his cult: Wenslow in Bedfordshire (meaning Woden's Barrow), Wednesfield in Staffordshire, and Wensley in Derbyshire (Woden's Grove).

It has been argued that the cult of Óðin was not indigenous to Scandinavia, but spread rather slowly from the south, and did not become significant until the Viking Age itself. But there is no doubt that he was a paramount god amongst the Germanic tribes with whom the Romans came into contact. The Romans identified Óðin with Mercury, and Tacitus wrote: 'Above all gods they worship Mercury, and count it no sin to win his favour on certain days with human sacrifices.' Tacitus also referred to gruesome rites that a tribe called the Semnones performed in sacred forest glades, when men were slaughtered and dedicated to *regnator omnium deus*—the supreme god, Wotan-Mercury.

There are numerous references by classical authorities to the Germanic custom of dedicating whole enemy armies to Óðin (a practice that was to be echoed in Viking times, when a spear would be thrown over the opposing host before battle was joined with the cry, 'Óðin owns you all!'). Mercury and Óðin were both psychopomps: 'leaders of souls'. In 105 BC the Cimbri, who had spilled out of Jutland, inflicted a heavy defeat on the Romans in the lower Rhône valley. Orosius described the victory rites in his *History of the World*: 'The enemy captured both camps and acquired a huge amount of booty. In fulfillment of a strange and unusual vow, they set about destroying everything they had got their hands on: clothing was ripped to pieces and thrown away, gold and silver was flung into the river, armour was hacked to pieces, horse-trappings were broken up, the horses themselves were drowned in whirlpools, and all prisoners were strung up on trees with nooses round their necks. Thus there was no booty for the victors and no mercy for the vanquished.'

Here we glimpse Óðin as Lord of the Slain, the god of battle: a savage god, to be propitiated by human blood. And evidence of this kind of sacrificial slaughter was discovered in 1950 in the Tollund bog in Jutland, when Danish archaeologists came across a number of bodies (dating from just before the Christian era) whose flesh had been mummified by the peat. They included the celebrated Tollund Man who was found naked except for a hat, belt and cloak, with a rope of two plaited leather thongs round his neck. He and several others had been ritually strangled or hanged. Most remarkably of all, on his face was a dying look not of horror and fear, but of serene acceptance, so that we must assume that he went willingly to his death.

A thousand years later, Adam of Bremen penned a remarkable description, albeit at second or third hand, of the great pagan cult-centre at Uppsala, in Sweden. The temple there, he wrote, was dedicated to Óðin, Thór, and Frey. Nearby stood a great tree with wide-spreading branches, always green both winter and summer (almost certainly an echo of the World Tree, Yggdrasil). Every ninth year it was the custom to hold

Óðin, the god of war, the god of guile in action.
Left: The standing man in the top section of this eleventh-century picture stone has been tentatively identified with Óðin, offering his spear to the old man seated on his right. There are several myths about Óðin sowing dissension amongst families; it is suggested that the old man is Ermaneric the Goth, who killed his own son (seated on the left) for alleged adultery with Ermaneric's young bride, Svanhild, who may be represented by the swan-like bird behind the younger man. In the Edda, Ermaneric had his son hanged—a frequent form of sacrifice to Óðin.
Below: Óðin mounted on his eight-legged steed, Sleipnir. This is the top panel from one of the Gotland picture-stones, dating from the ninth century. The structure on the left is thought to represent Valhöll, the Hall of the Slain, where Óðin's champions fought and feasted in preparation for the doom of the world

a great general festival of all the provinces in Sweden, which lasted for nine days. 'The sacrifice is of this nature: of every living thing that is male, they offer nine heads, with the blood of which it is customary to placate gods of this sort. The bodies they hang in the sacred grove that adjoins the temple. Now this grove is so sacred in the eyes of the heathen that each and every tree in it is believed divine because of the death or putrefaction of the victims. . . . On each day they offer a man along with other living beings in such number that in the course of the nine days they will have made offerings of seventy-two creatures.'

The ritual aspect of the cult, with its insistence on the figure nine, is illuminated by one of the most enigmatic passages in the Óðin mythology. It is the account of Óðin's own ritual hanging, as related in one of the mythological poems in the *Elder Edda*, the *Hávamál* (*Words of the High One*). It represents a new and deeper dimension—the sacrifice of Óðin to Óðin himself in his search for the secret wisdom of the dead:

> I know that I hung
> On the windswept tree
> For nine whole nights,
> Pierced by the spear
> And given to Óðin:
> Myself given to myself
> On that tree
> Whose roots
> No one knows.
>
> They gave me not bread
> Nor drink from the horn;
> Into the depths I peered,
> I grasped the runes,
> Screaming I grasped them,
> And then fell back.

The tree was assuredly the World Tree, Yggdrasil and the spear with which he was gashed was assuredly his own spear, Gungnir. This spear had been forged by the dwarves and determined the outcome of battle by direction it took over the field of combat. The runes grasped by the god represented the magical knowledge of the occult which could only be obtained from the dead themselves. Many commentators have seen Christian parallels in this powerful and dramatic image, of the young god suffering the supreme sacrifice on a tree, gashed with a spear and crying out in agony at the moment of fulfillment. But it springs equally from the ancient idea of shamanism and sorcery, whereby the initiate has to suffer fearful self-inflicted tortures in his quest for knowledge. The search for knowledge is a constant theme in the Óðin mythology. Óðin would wrench knowledge from men who died on the gallows by carving and painting such runes that the dead could talk to him. He would go down into the Otherworld and force dead sibyls to speak—it was one such who told him the destiny of the world as it appears in *Völuspá* (*The Sibyl's Prophecy*). Óðin would also seek wisdom from his implacable foes, the giants. The wisest of these was the giant Mímir, who tended the fount of wisdom that lay at one of the roots of Yggdrasil. The myths about Mímir are confused. In his youth, Óðin is said to have gone to Mímir and asked for a drink from the fount of wisdom, but to gain it he had to sacrifice one of his eyes. Mímir is also said to have been one of the hostages that the Æsir sent to the Vanir at the end of the war of the gods. The Vanir later beheaded him, but Óðin pickled the head with herbs and kept it alive, so that it could whisper to him the secrets of the future. In his restless search for foreknowledge, Óðin mastered the blackest arts of sorcery whereby he could see into the future and cause death and destruction. It was a form of

Birds are repeated symbols in Viking art, often associated with Óðin.

Left: Mounted warrior who is probably Óðin with his spear Gungnir, accompanied by two birds—the ravens Huginn (Mind) and Muninn (Memory). Ravens brought Óðin news from all over the world; they were also the carrion-birds of the battlefield. This representation is from a helmet-plate found in the cemetery at Vendel, Sweden, and dating from the seventh century.

Below left: Bronze bird-like mask, used as a mount for the top of a staff, dating from the Late Bronze Age.

Below: Bird-clasp in gilded bronze from Jelling in Denmark, dating from the Viking period

magic and wizardry that involved the most depraved practices.

His search for knowledge, for information, was ceaseless. From his throne in Ásgarð he could see out over all the world. On his shoulders perched his constant companions, two ravens called Huginn and Muninn (Mind and Memory). Snorri Sturluson wrote: 'They sit on his shoulders and whisper into his ear every scrap of news they see or hear. At the crack of dawn he sends them off to fly right round the world, and they are back by breakfast-time. This is the source of much of his knowledge, and this is why men call him the Raven-god.'

Ravens were also scavengers of the battlefield, as were the wolf and the eagle, the other creature symbols of Óðin. They bring us back to the primary source of Óðin-worship, as Lord of the Slain, the god of war. With his occult foreknowledge of the doom that

Above and right: Óðin's birds—a pair of gilt-bronze harness mounts from Gotland. The exaggerated beaks and talons emphasize the ferocity of the eagles, which were widely associated with the cult of Óðin. This motif is found in the finds from many different areas, including the seventh-century Sutton Hoo ship-burial in England, where Anglo-Saxon craftsmen had evidently used Swedish designs for their decorative themes

awaited the world, Óðin used his divine powers of life and death to build up an army of hand-picked warriors for the final battle at Ragnarök. Thus, the god's favour could manifest itself on the battlefield in defeat and death, since this meant that the victim would join this *élite* host of champions. This explained the apparent treachery with which Óðin treated men to whom he had promised victory, and justified the brutal uncertainties of war.

Thus death on the battlefield was predestined, and the noblest and bravest warriors would be picked out by Óðin's Amazonian handmaidens, the flying Valkyries, and ushered by them to Óðin's great hall in Ásgarð, Valhöll, the Hall of the Slain (wrongly transliterated into English in its genitive plural form as 'Valhalla'). Valhöll was a great palace with a structure somewhat reminiscent of the Roman Colosseum and with no fewer than 640 doorways. Through each doorway 960 champions could march shoulder to shoulder. Its rafters were spear-shafts, its tiles were shields of gold, its benches were strewn with coats of mail. A wolf lurked at the western door, an eagle hovered overhead. Here the fallen champions spent all day gaming and fighting one another, all former enmities and alliances forgotten in the fierce joy of battle. At the end of each day the dead and the wounded were all healed, so that they could spend all night feasting on succulent pork stew from an everlasting boar whose flesh never gave out, and drinking copious mead from the udders of a magic goat. The handmaids who kept the ale-horns brimming were off-duty Valkyries. Óðin himself sat apart and ate nothing; he gave all his food to his two pet wolves, and himself drank only wine.

Valhöll was the archetypal warrior paradise, an endless roistering orgy of fighting and feasting, with a suggestion of call-girls thrown in! It was essentially a Viking fantasy, and there is little evidence that it was widely believed except in the specialized world of the Viking chieftains and their followers. It is elegantly and lavishly expressed in the poetry of the age, but the poetry itself was as esoteric as the life-style of the Vikings and their belief in Óðin.

Óðin was the patron god of poetry as well as the god of battle and this other major attribute is reflected in another clutch of myths. This helps to explain why so much information about Óðin has survived, for the court-poets of the Viking Age were Óðin's publicists to a man. Snorri Sturluson explains how Óðin originally got his hands on the magic mead of inspiration. It was accomplished by deceit and treachery, as were so many of Óðin's achievements, and the story goes back to the war between the Æsir and the Vanir. When the two tribes of gods made peace, they signified their pact by spitting into a jar. From this joint spittle the gods fashioned a human figure. He was called Kvasir, and was the wisest of all living creatures. But during his travels round the world, imparting wisdom to all, he was secretly murdered by two dwarves who filled three casks with his blood; this blood they mixed with honey, and from it they brewed the magic potion of poetry and learning. Later, in revenge for another killing, a giant called Suttung forced the dwarves to ransom their lives by giving up the mead, which Suttung then stored away in his mountain dwelling under the care of his daughter, Gunnlöð. Now Óðin enters the story. In one of his many disguises he took service with Suttung's brother, and demanded a drink of Suttung's mead as his wages. When Suttung refused, Óðin bored a hole in the mountain where the mead was kept, and then changed into the form of a serpent and crawled through the hole. Once inside, he seduced Suttung's daughter and made love to her for three nights. As a reward, she granted him three drinks of the mead. In three deep draughts he emptied the three casks of mead and then, leaving Gunnlöð in tears, he changed into the form of an eagle and flew off towards Ásgarð. Suttung, enraged by the theft, transformed himself into an eagle too, and set off in hot pursuit. When the gods saw Óðin approaching, they set out vats by the walls of Ásgarð, and Óðin, with Suttung right on his tail, regurgitated the precious mead into the vats before Suttung could catch him. A charming footnote to the story adds that some of the mead splashed from the vats and fell outside the walls of Ásgarð. This is the less heady brew of inspiration that poetasters and writers of doggerel receive.

Such was the god whom the poets and their patrons, the Viking chieftains of Scandinavia, worshipped above all others. He was in no way an attractive or sympathetic god; he was cruel, sinister, fickle. He travelled widely round the world in disguise, grey-bearded and wearing an old blue cloak and a wide-brimmed hat, one-eyed and baleful. Wherever he went, he stirred up trouble and distress, setting kings and kinsmen at loggerheads in order to be able to reap a harvest of fallen warriors for Valhöll. Modern psychology might call him a psychopath.

But in all his doings, his ultimate purpose was to try to fend off the terrible destiny that he knew awaited the world of men and gods. No trick was too treacherous, no battle too bloody, no sacrifice too excessive to help fortify the world against the coming encounter, the Armageddon of paganism, and Óðin was thus beyond the normal human concepts of good and evil.

To his followers he imparted a dark and brooding pessimism, but with it he gave the courage to shrug it off. In battle, men were imbued with an ecstasy of combat that made them seem impervious to injury or pain. They became berserks who gnawed the rims of their shields and howled and fought like wild beasts. To his aristocratic worshippers, like King Eric Blood-Axe of Norway, he revealed the qualities required by a Viking adventurer; how to be brave, unscrupulous,

crafty, and murderous. When Eric Blood-Axe fell in battle in England in 954, after his tenure of the Norse throne in York, he was accorded a particularly splendid welcome in Valhöll.

Óðin had a wife, called Frigg, whose name is commemorated in the week-day Friday (Anglo-Saxon *Frigedæg*). Originally, Frigg seems to have been confused with Jörð (Earth); her name is related to the Old Icelandic verb *frjá*, meaning 'to love', and she was the goddess of domestic, conjugal love. Not that she was a model of fidelity; indeed, her morals are depicted as being particularly lax, and she enjoyed frequent altercations with her husband in many of which she prevailed. There is no surviving evidence of a specific cult of Frigg in Scandinavia, but her position in the hierarchy as wife of Óðin, and therefore the mother of the gods, suggests a great antiquity as an Earth Mother in Germanic mythology.

storm
and
harvest

thór, frey, freyja:
gods of the earth and sky

Although Óðin was portrayed by the poets of the Viking Age as All-Father, the most widely venerated of the gods of the Norse pantheon was not Óðin, but Thór.

Thór was pre-eminently the God of Thunder (Germanic *Thonar*, Anglo-Saxon *Thunor*), just like Zeus and Jupiter, with whom the Romans equated him; and his name is still commemorated in English by the week-day Thursday and in French by *Jeudi* (*Jovis dies*). He was god of the sky, ruler of storms and tempests, wielder of thunderbolts, and was seen as a huge red-haired man, with a red beard, beetling red eyebrows, and blazing eyes. He rode the heavens in a chariot drawn by two sacred goats, and at his passage thunder rumbled and crashed, the earth quaked, and lightning cracked.

Left: Sogne Fjord in Norway, dramatically lit as the sun breaks through the storm clouds associated with Thór, the god of thunder

67

Right and below: Thór is a far more approachable and understandable figure than the mysterious god, Óðin. He wielded great power among the gods and his strong robust nature made him the favoured deity of the ordinary people of Viking times. The tenth-century bronze image, below, is from Iceland and shows him in characteristic pose grasping his hammer. The more enigmatic Viking Age amber figure from Denmark, right, shows a similar pose and may also be a representation of the god

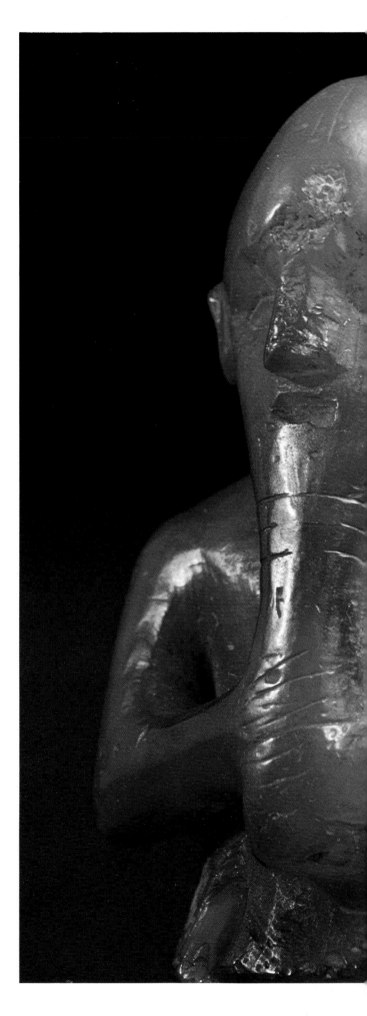

Many scholars have noted the extraordinary resemblance between Thór and the Vedic storm-god, Indra.

In the later literary myths, Thór frequently emerges as a comic rather than as a serious figure: big, bluff and boisterous, Gargantuan in appetite but not overburdened with intelligence. Indeed, the professional court-poets of the Viking world tended to sneer at him when comparing him to Óðin:

> Óðin has earls
> Who fall in battle,
> But Thór has the race of slaves.

But all the evidence suggests that Thór was revered above Óðin in daily life. In temples where Óðin, Frey and Thór were worshipped jointly it was Thór who was granted place of honour in the middle. When Adam of Bremen described the great temple at Uppsala he wrote that 'the mightiest of them, Thór, occupies a throne in the middle of the chamber; Wodan and Fricco [Frey] have places on either side . . . Thór, they say, presides over the air, and governs the thunder and lightning, the winds and rains, fair weather and crops.'

The reference to 'crops' is illuminating, because Thór had originally been an earth-god, a god of fertility and fruitfulness. He was said to be the first-born son of Óðin and Jörð (Mother Earth), and his wife, Sif, had the attributes of a northern fertility goddess, with waving golden hair that had been fashioned by the dwarves. In Sweden there are place-names echoing ancient memories of Thór as an earth-god. Although there is little evidence of a fertility cult associated with Thór in the Viking Age, his sacred emblem, the hammer, was used to hallow weddings and funerals and people carried his amulet as a good-luck charm. The Viking poets were right in one respect: Thór was the god of the ordinary people, the farmers, the peasants, the oarsmen, the settlers, the pioneers, and he was invoked also as a protection against the autocratic chieftains themselves and their aristocratic god, Óðin.

It was as Lord Protector that Thór ruled supreme. His function in the pantheon was that of the Guardian of the World, both of gods and men. He was immensely powerful and brave, wise and noble, and it was to him that men turned in times of stress, just as the gods themselves did. He was the implacable foe of the giants who constantly menaced the world order and of the World Serpent that lay coiled round the world in the depths of Ocean. Most of his time seems to have been spent making ferocious assaults on the fastnesses of these enemies.

In the mythology, he is said to have owned three treasured possessions. The first was a magic belt, Megingjarðar (Strength-Increaser), which doubled his divine strength when he girded himself with it. The second was a pair of iron gauntlets with which to grasp and shatter rocks. He also wore them to wield his third and most prized possession, the greatest of all the treasures of Ásgarð, his mighty hammer, Mjöllnir. It was a short-handled weapon (the dwarf who forged it had been interrupted in his work by a gnat which stung him on the eyelid!) which could be swung or thrown, and which always returned to his hand like a boomerang. Its name is associated etymologically with crushing or with lightning—literally, a thunderbolt. This was the weapon with which Thór maintained the stability of the world and kept the forces of chaos in check.

There are several mythological lays in the *Elder Edda* which tell entertaining stories of Thór's conflicts with the giants. Cracking giant heads was Thór's favourite pastime. Snorri Sturlu·son summarized them in his own *Prose Edda*. One time, when Thór was 'out east' killing giants, another giant called Hrungnir had the effrontery to come to Ásgarð uninvited; he became exceedingly drunk, and boasted that he would level Ásgarð to the ground and carry off the most beautiful of the goddesses. The Æsir, in growing alarm, called upon Thór, and, in a twinkling, Thór was standing in the hall brandishing his hammer and fuming with rage. Hrungnir pointed out that he was unarmed—he had left his celebrated shield and whetstone at home—but that he would be happy to meet Thór in single combat any time he wished. The duel was arranged. Hrungnir's fellow-giants were a little apprehensive about it: Hrungnir was the strongest of them, and if he were felled, the others could expect little mercy from Thór. So they made a decoy, a clay giant nine leagues tall and measuring three leagues across the chest. Hrungnir himself had a head made of stone and a great stone shield; his whetstone was a mighty weapon which he carried on his shoulder.

The plan was that Thór's attention would be distracted by the clay giant long enough for Hrungnir to deal with him. But Thór had a companion who spied on the giants, and indulged a little ploy of his own: he told Hrungnir that it was useless to hold his shield out in front of him for Thór had seen him and was planning to attack him from under the ground. So Hrungnir put his shield on the ground and stood on it, taking hold of his whetstone with both hands.

Now Thór arrived in a tumult of thunder and lightning. His companion made straight for the clay giant who crumbled at once. Meanwhile Thór whirled his mighty hammer and hurled it at Hrungnir. Hrungnir saw it coming, and threw his whetstone in return. It met the hammer in midflight and shattered, and fragments from it struck Thór, embedding themselves in his head so that he fell to the ground. But the hammer continued on its deadly way and hit Hrungnir squarely on his stone forehead, crushing his head to powder, and Hrungnir fell dead across the prostrate Thór. None of the gods could lift the giant's leg to get Thór out from under him, until Thór's infant son arrived. The child's

name was Magni (Might), and though he was only three days old at the time, he tossed the leg effortlessly to one side and said, 'What a pity I arrived so late, father; I would have put paid to this giant with my bare fists if I had got at him.' Thór now recovered his senses, and left the field in triumph, with nothing worse than a headache and some bits of whetstone still embedded in his skull.

This rumbustious narrative is typical of the late stories about Thór. His most celebrated journey to the land of the giants, his visit to the castle of Útgarðar-Loki, a giant with great magical powers, has far more subtle allegorical overtones.

After Thór and his companions had crossed Ocean, they found themselves in a deep forest as night was falling. They came to a huge hall, with a great door spanning the whole gable end, and here they bedded down. That night they were woken up by a severe

earthquake, accompanied by loud rumblings, and the house shuddered and shook. This went on all night, while Thór stood guard over his companions. At first light Thór went outside, and there, a little way off in the forest, he saw an enormous giant lying asleep and snoring loudly. The snoring explained the earthquake—and the vast 'hall' had merely been the giant's discarded glove. Thór was somewhat annoyed, and after an altercation the following night, when the giant was once again fast asleep, Thór determined to kill him. Seizing Mjöllnir in both hands, he crashed it down on the giant's skull. The giant woke up and merely asked if a leaf had fallen on his head, soon dropping off to sleep again. Thór, abashed, lay down to sleep, but soon the giant's snores were shaking the forest again, until Thór could stand it no longer. He went over and dealt the giant an even fiercer blow on the head, sinking the face of the hammer into the skull. This time the giant woke

and said, 'What's up? Was that an acorn falling on my head?' Just before dawn Thór tried once again; leaping at the giant, he swung Mjöllnir with all his might at the giant's temple. The hammer sank in right up to the handle, but the giant merely sat up and rubbed his cheek, complaining that some birds must have showered him with twigs from the branches above.

Eventually they all reached the stronghold of Útgarðar-Loki. The giant, who was Útgarðar-Loki in disguise, warned them not to put on airs because Útgarðar-Loki and his men would not stand for any bragging from midgets like them. Once inside, dwarfed by their hosts, they were challenged to show their skill. One of Thór's companions challenged all-comers to an eating competition. He and his opponent, Logi, ate their way down a long trough of meat and met at the middle, but whereas Thór's companion had only eaten the meat, his opponent, whose name meant Wildfire,

Left and above: The simplest and most enduring symbol of Viking mythology – Thór's hammer, Mjöllnir. Its name is associated with a thunderbolt and with this weapon Thór defended the order of the gods against their foes. The simple tenth-century silver hammer, above left, comes from Uppland, Sweden. It is typical of the amulets worn as lucky charms. The brilliant silver work in the head of the hammer, left, was done in the Viking period and shows the stark, staring eyes associated with Thór. The hammer from Iceland, above, also made in the tenth century, shows how Christian symbolism, in the shape of the cross, was gradually incorporated into Viking artefacts
Right: An eighth-century bronze plaque from Sweden showing Thór and a sea-giant fishing for the World Serpent. Though the World Serpent took the bait, Thór's companion was so terrified at the sight of the monster that he cut him free – a mistake that was to have disastrous consequences at Ragnarök

was adjudged the winner because he had consumed not only the meat but the bones and even the trough itself. Thór's other companion, Thjálfi ('Trained'), offered to take on anyone at foot-racing, but no matter how fast he sprinted, he was utterly beaten by Útgarðar-Loki's pageboy, Hugi, whose name meant Thought.

When it came to Thór's turn, he said he would prefer a drinking contest. A great horn was brought in, which, said Útgarðar-Loki, most of his own men could empty at one draught, although some took two. Thór thought the horn rather long, but he was thirsty and took a mighty swig at it. When his breath gave out, he saw that the level in the horn had hardly dropped. He took another huge draught, but the level dropped even less, and the giants jeered. In a rage, Thór rammed the horn into his mouth and drank for dear life. When he looked into the horn, however, he saw that the level had gone down only a tiny bit, and with that he gave up.

By now, Thór's temper was running very high, and he challenged anyone in the hall to wrestle with him. Útgarðar-Loki claimed that his men would consider it beneath their dignity to wrestle with such a puny fellow, and he summoned his old nurse instead. Her name was Elli. The old crone came hobbling into the hall ready to wrestle with Thór. The harder Thór fought, the firmer she stood, until Thór himself missed his footing and was forced down onto one knee.

Next morning, Thór left the giant's castle in chastened mood after his humiliating experience. As he reached the gate, however, the giant revealed that Thór had proved himself much mightier than it had seemed: the three hammer-blows he had delivered had, in fact, fallen upon a mountain and had gouged three deep valleys; the end of the horn from which Thór had drunk had been connected to the sea, whose level had fallen by several feet, causing the tides to start; and the old crone, Elli, with whom he had wrestled had been Old Age, whom no one, however strong, could ever overcome.

In a rage, Thór seized his hammer and raised it for a swing. But Útgarðar-Loki had vanished, and so had the towering battlements of his castle. There was nothing to be seen but a broad and pleasant plain.

Thór's arch-enemy was Miðgarðsorm, the World Serpent, which lay curled round the earth in the depths of Ocean, a lurking evil that would overwhelm the world at Ragnarök. One day Thór, disguised as a youth, went fishing with the sea-giant Hýmir. As bait he took the head of an ox, which he flung out on his line. The serpent took the bait, and Thór started heaving on the line, but the serpent struggled so vehemently that Thór's

Right: The remarkable gold work in this Migration Period bracteate (pendant) from Sweden is typical of the period. Such bracteates were worn on the chest suspended from the neck as magical amulets and bore various symbols including swastikas and animal figures

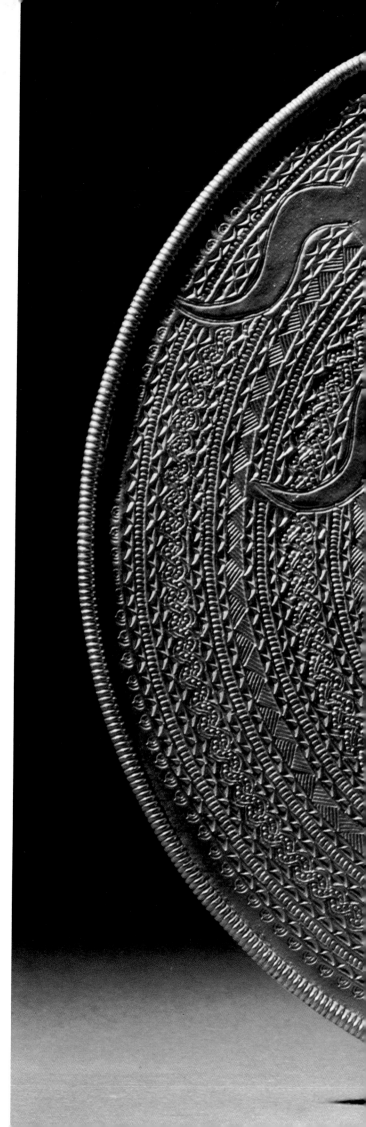

Above: Viking period pendant from Sweden representing the goddess Freyja, twin sister to Frey, and a figure of great lasciviousness and beauty. Around her shoulders is the fabulous Brísingamen, the necklace made for her by the dwarves
Opposite page, above: Bronze matrix from Uppland, Sweden, made in the seventh century and used in the manufacture of plaques for the adornment of helmets. The helmets worn by the warriors are topped by the figures of boars – animals constantly associated with Frey
Opposite page, below: Frey, god of fertility, represented by an eleventh-century bronze figurine from Sweden. Frey was often shown with penis erect, symbolizing his potency, and sacrifice was made to him at weddings

fists were smashed against the gunnel. Thór now grew enraged and, summoning all his strength, he pulled so hard that his feet went right through the bottom of the boat and his legs stretched until he was standing on the sea bed.

Hand over hand, he hauled in the serpent, and when the serpent broke surface it was a blood-curdling sight, glaring at Thór and spewing venom. The giant Hýmir blenched with terror, and then, as Thór snatched up his hammer and raised it aloft to crush the serpent's head, the giant fumbled for his bait-knife and chopped off the line against the gunnel. The serpent sank back into the sea. In fury, Thór hurled his hammer at the serpent without avail, swung a fist at Hýmir that knocked him overboard, and then waded ashore.

This failure to land the World Serpent was to prove costly. At Ragnarök, the 'one that got away' would rise against the world and drown it, and Thór and the serpent would kill each other in a last titanic duel.

All the mythological stories emphasize Thór's brute strength, his bluff, downright attitude, and his prowess against the dreaded giants. His popularity seems to have increased steadily as paganism waned in the Viking Age. Farmers and seamen invoked him; indeed, it is reported of Helgi the Lean, one of the first settlers in Iceland late in the ninth century, that 'he believed in Christ, but invoked Thór on sea-journeys and in moments of stress'. It was Thór who guided Helgi to the place where he should settle in Iceland, but when Helgi reached the appointed place, in the north of Iceland, he called it Kristness. It appears that Thór was very much the patron god of the Icelandic settlement; at that time, Christianity and paganism could live together quite harmoniously in Iceland, and in one individual. When serious attempts were made to evangelize Iceland in the last decade of the tenth century, it was Thór who was invoked to oppose the new religion. *Njál's Saga* records a meeting between the missionary Thangbrand and an Icelandic poetess, after Thangbrand's ship was wrecked. The poetess claimed triumphantly that it was Thór who had smashed the ship and that Christ had been helpless to save it.

The third of the major trinity of the Norse pantheon was the fertility god Frey, closely associated with his twin sister, Freyja. They were the children of one of the Vanir tribe of gods, Njörð, who had joined the Æsir as a hostage after the primeval war between the gods.

Njörð seems to have been a very ancient god, deeply rooted in Germanic mythology. His name is closely related to that of the goddess Nerthus (Mother Earth), who was worshipped among the Angles and other Germanic tribes on the west coast of the Baltic at the start of the Christian era. Tacitus in his *Germania* (*c*. AD 100) described her cult in great detail:
'None of these tribes is particularly noteworthy, except for their common worship of Nerthus, or Mother Earth. They believe that she intercedes in human affairs,

and travels through the nations in her wagon. In an island of the Ocean there is a sacred grove, within which stands a chariot covered with a cloth, which none but the priest may touch. The priest can feel the presence of the goddess in this holy place. When she goes out in her wagon drawn by oxen, he attends her with the utmost reverence. A season of rejoicing and festivity reigns everywhere the goddess honours with her presence; all weapons are laid aside and locked away, no one goes to war; peace and quiet are known and welcomed then, and only then, until the goddess wearies of the society of mortals and is restored to her temple by the priest. Afterwards the wagon, the cloth and even (believe it or not) the goddess herself are washed and purified in a secret lake. This rite is performed by slaves, who are immediately afterwards drowned in the lake. Hence there arises a holy terror and a pious reluctance to know more of that which is seen only by eyes doomed to death.'

Despite the difference of sex, no one doubts that Nerthus and Njörð were the same deity, or aspects of the same deity. According to Snorri Sturluson, Njörð was one of the ancestral divine kings of the Swedes, venerated as a ruler of peace and plenty, and as the father of Frey. Gradually, Frey usurped his father's functions as a fertility god, and in the Norse pantheon Njörð had been relegated to a minor sea-god, although the evidence of place-names suggests that the worship of Njörð throughout Scandinavia was both ancient and widespread.

Snorri Sturluson wrote of Njörð in *Gylfaginning*: 'The third god is the one named Njörð. He lives in heaven in the place called Nóatún [Anchorage]. He rules the winds, and can still the sea and quench fire. He should be invoked for sea-journeys and fishing-luck; he is so wealthy and rich in livestock that he can grant either land or chattels to those who ask for them.'

Although he had become a patron god of fishermen and deep-sea sailors by Viking times, echoes of his original function as a fertility god were still to be found in the story of his marriage. It came about because a giant called Thjazi kidnapped one of the goddesses of Ásgarð, Iðunn, who looked after the apples of immortality which kept the gods young. The Æsir got their revenge by killing Thjazi and recovering the golden apples, but his daughter, Skaði (Harm), came rushing down from the mountains of Giantland bent on vengeance. As compensation for her father's death, the Æsir offered her a husband from among their number. The only condition they made was that she could make her choice only from the gods' legs! Skaði picked the handsomest pair of legs she saw, convinced they must belong to the shining god Baldur, but it turned out to be Njörð of Nóatún.

So a Frost Giantess married a fertility god: winter married spring. The union was evidently not a happy

one. Njörð wanted to live by the sea, Skaði wanted to live in the mountains of Giantland. They tried to compromise by spending nine nights in each other's home in turn, but Njörð could not stand the sound of the howling of wolves in the snow and Skaði could not stand the sound of seagulls mewing, so the marriage broke up.

Prior to the marriage with Skaði, Njörð had begotten two children (by his own sister, the sources suggest). These were the twins, Frey and Freyja. Snorri Sturluson described them thus: 'They [are] beautiful and mighty. Frey is the noblest of the gods. He controls the rain and the sunshine and therefore the natural increase of the earth, and it is good to call upon him for fruitful seasons and for peace. He also controls the good fortunes of men. Likewise, Freyja is the most excellent of the goddesses . . . Her palace is called Sessrúmnir [Roomy]. On her journeys, she sits in a wagon drawn by two cats. She is the most favourable one for men to call upon . . . She is well pleased with love-songs; on her it is good to call upon in affairs of the heart.'

Their names meant, simply, 'Lord' and 'Lady'—twin aspects of the fertility cult. Freyja was the loveliest and most lascivious of the goddesses, the equivalent of Venus and Aphrodite. The giants lusted after her, while she lusted after both men and riches. Her celebrated necklace, the Brísing treasure, was made for her by the dwarves at the expense, it is suggested, of her chastity. She was the mistress of Óðin for a time.

There is little evidence of Freyja-worship in Norse times; rather, she was simply a counterpart of her brother. It was Frey who was the chief god of fertility in the late pagan period; he was the paramount god of the Swedes, and the divine ancestor of their kings. The great temple at Uppsala was said to have been built by Frey when he made it his chief seat. Adam of Bremen reported in the eleventh century that his wooden image at Uppsala was equipped with a gigantic penis, symbolizing his powers of fertility and prosperous increase, and that the Swedes made sacrifices to him at weddings: 'He bestows peace and pleasure on mortals.' The animal most sacred to Frey was the boar, while his sister Freyja was identified with the sow: twin symbols of fecundity. Early Swedish kings wore helmets with boars depicted on them, no doubt associated with Frey's prize possession, the boar Gullinbursti (Gold-Bristled), which had been fashioned by the dwarves and could outrun any horse. The stallion was also particularly associated with Frey. In the Icelandic *Hrafnkel's Saga,* Hrafnkel (Frey's Priest) dedicates his horse Freyfaxi to Frey, and kills a man who dared to ride him without permission.

In Norse mythology, Frey is remembered as a symbol of the divine marriage between the sky and the earth that produces spring. There is only one story about Frey in the mythological lays of the Edda. Like his father Njörð, Frey married a giantess, and the story of his

Left: These tiny gold foils from Uppland, Sweden, were probably used as amulets in association with fertility rites. Each shows a couple embracing who have been identified as Frey and Gerð
Below: Sandstone lid of a Bronze Age cremation urn from Denmark with obvious fertility symbolism. The two figures advancing towards one another are surrounded by a necklace formed from a corn motif which is repeated behind the female figure. This crude but forceful image pre-dates the clever workmanship of the gold foil, left, by hundreds of years, but the underlying theme has remained the same

wooing is told in a magnificent love-poem called *Skírnismál*.

One day, Frey climbed onto Óðin's throne and looked out over all the worlds. To the north, in Giant-land, he caught sight of a beautiful maiden standing by her father's hall. This was the maiden Gerð (Field), the daughter of a mountain-giant. Her arms were so dazzlingly bright that when she raised them to unlatch the door, their radiance illumined the earth and sky and sea. Frey was overcome with desire for her, and grew so lovesick that he could neither eat nor sleep, and no one dared speak to him. Eventually he asked his servant, Skírnir (The Bright One), to go and woo her on his behalf, and sent him off to the land of the Frost Giants with his own magic sword, which could fight by itself, and a horse which could carry him through the darkness and the enchanted flames of the Otherworld. It was a long and dangerous journey, and the wooing at the end of it proved equally difficult. First, Skírnir offered Gerð the eleven golden apples of immortality, but she refused to accept them. Then he offered her one of Óðin's most prized possessions, the magic arm-ring Draupnir, which had the power of producing eight similar rings every ninth night. But still Gerð refused to accept Frey's suit. Skírnir now resorted to threats: he would cut off her head with the magic sword, and kill her father too; he would turn her into an old hag with his magic wand. But even such dreadful threats proved unavailing; Gerð had no fear of the wrath of the gods, so Skírnir now had to fall back on the threat of dire curses. She would waste away like a dry thistle. Her flesh would become repulsive to her and to all men. She would be an outcast and forced to drink goat's piss. She would be racked with the torments of unfulfilled longing for repulsive three-headed Frost-Giants. She would be plagued by perversions and unbridled lusts. It was this final threat that won the maiden over: Gerð relented, and agreed to marry Frey. 'When?' asked Skírnir. She replied that in nine days' time she would meet Frey in the windless grove called Barri (Barley) and become his bride. When Frey heard the news he cried out:

> One night is long,
> Two are longer,
> How can I endure for three?
> Often a month
> Seemed to me shorter
> Than half this night of longing.

Frey got his bride, but in the wooing he lost his magic sword, so that when he faced the giant Surt at Ragnarök he was defenceless, and fell.

The story has all the classic elements of a seasonal fertility myth, the spring melting of the ice-hearted earth, and it seems to have been played out in the Frey-cult with scenes of sacred and ritualized intercourse.

loki and baldur

the father of lies and the shining god

Above: The writhing convolutions of evil, of the mischief wrought by Loki, are echoed in the curious 'gripping-beasts' motif of the carvings on the stem and stern of the Oseberg ship. These extraordinary creatures have beards and pigtails, popping eyes, and expressions of pained concentration; their bodies have spindly limbs with accentuated, pear-shaped thighs and biceps, and they grip each other with both hands and feet to form an intricate pattern of catch-as-catch-can

Left: Loki was hermaphroditic, and one of his offspring was the magic eight-legged steed, Sleipnir, depicted here on a Gotland picture stone. Sleipnir, who later became Óðin's horse, was conceived when Loki, in the guise of a mare, lured away the stallion owned by a giant who was repairing the walls of Ásgarð, in order to ensure that the work should not be finished and the gods would not have to pay the contract they had agreed

Loki is one of the most intriguing figures in the Norse pantheon. There is no evidence to suggest that he ever inspired a cult, or was worshipped as a god. He had no relationship at all with the world of men, and though he lived in Ásgarð among the gods, he was probably not of divine origin himself. The myths about him are inconsistent; in the oldest traditions he was the son of a giant, yet somehow became a close companion of the gods—he even entered into a pact of blood-brotherhood with Óðin. It has been suggested that the name 'Loki' is cognate with Latin *lux*, meaning 'light', and hence with Lucifer; in fact, in the later traditions from the Viking Age Loki does appear in a semi-Satanic guise. Generally, his position amongst the gods and his attitude towards them is ambiguous: he is both ally and foe.

Snorri Sturluson was well aware of the complexity of this character and his position: 'There is yet another to be counted amongst the Æsir, whom some call the slander-bearer of the gods, the father of lies, and the disgrace of all gods and men. He is called Loki or Lopt [Air, Sky-Traveller], the son of the giant Fárbauti [Cruel Smiter] . . . Loki is handsome to look upon, but evil of temper and extremely fickle in manner. He excels all others in guile and slyness, and resorts to wiles in everything. Time and again he brought the gods into grave trouble, but usually he also rescued them by his wiles.'

There is a curious dualism here, and some commentators have seen Loki as a fire-spirit, sometimes the friend but potentially the foe of the world, handsome but treacherous, useful but dangerous. He was essentially a literary personification. According to the earliest sources his misadventures are caused by his own weaknesses. He is a coward, and vulnerable to the threats and pressures of the giants, who frequently blackmail him into putting the gods into difficult situations from which, as a rule, he later manages to extricate them by his wiles. In the later traditions, however, where his 'Satanic' qualities are emphasized, he is used as a means of reconciling the apparent contradictions of good and evil co-existing among the gods in Ásgarð. It is Loki, in fact, who precipitates Ragnarök, and who thus emerges as the implacable enemy of the gods and the world.

One story will suffice to illustrate the early concept of his fecklessness and cowardice—and his capacity to recover. It is a justly celebrated story, contained in one of the poems of the *Elder Edda*, the *Þrymskviða* (*Thrym's Lay*). The story tells how Thór lost and regained his hammer, with Loki's help.

One morning Thór woke up in Ásgarð to find that his mighty hammer, Mjöllnir, was missing. His anguish knew no bounds, and he bellowed for Loki to tell him the news. (In other sources there is a suggestion that it was Loki himself who had stolen the hammer and given it to Thór's traditional enemies, the giants.) Loki was sent off to Giantland to seek the hammer, wearing Freyja's magic flying feather-coat. There he met Thrym, the king of Giantland, sitting on a mound plaiting leashes of gold for his hounds and trimming the manes of his horses. Thrym told him that he had hidden Thór's hammer deep underground, and would only give it back if he were given Freyja to wife.

When Thór heard the news he charged into Freyja's bower and ordered her to put on the bridal veil at once and drive with him to Giantland. But Freyja flew into a rage at the suggestion, and refused to marry the giant. The gods met in council, and it was suggested by Heimdall that Thór himself should dress up as the bride and go and fetch the hammer. Thór was suitably reluctant to be thought a sissy, but was eventually persuaded when Loki offered to accompany him as his bridesmaid. Heavily disguised in bridal clothes, the unlikely pair drove off to Giantland in the goat-drawn chariot with rumbles of thunder and flashes of lightning.

There was great rejoicing in Giantland when the chariot was sighted, and the bridal feast was set. The 'bride', whose gargantuan appetite was a recurring feature of the myths, promptly wolfed down a whole ox and eight salmon, washed down with three tuns of mead. In some surprise, Thrym remarked that he had never before seen a maiden with such a voracious appetite and thirst, but Loki slyly accounted for this by saying that Freyja had been so excited at the prospect of the wedding that she had neither eaten nor drunk for a week. Satisfied by this explanation, Thrym tried to steal a kiss, and lifted the bride's veil, only to be startled by the terrible blazing eyes that glared at him. Loki had to step in quickly once again to explain that Freyja's eyes were fiery because she had not slept for a week in anticipation of the wedding. Finally, Thrym called for the wedding to be consecrated in the traditional way, with Thór's hammer being laid in the bride's lap while bride and bridegroom made their vows. This was the moment Thór had been waiting for. As soon as he felt the haft of Mjöllnir within his grasp his heart laughed in his breast and he started to lay about Thrym in his usual manner, killing him with all his giant family and all the wedding guests before returning to Ásgarð in triumph.

Alone among the denizens of Ásgarð, Loki was imbued with wit and a mordant sense of humour. One of the lays in the *Elder Edda* is called *Lokasenna* (*Loki's Taunting*), and tells the story of a divine dinner-party that got out of hand. All the gods and goddesses were present, except Thór, who was away killing giants. Loki had violated the sanctuary of the hall by killing one of the servants and was thrown out. Eventually he was allowed back in, however, and he celebrated his return by hurling abuse at all the gods in turn. Óðin was called a transvestite who dabbled in sorcery, and who often awarded victory in battle to cowards instead of to the brave. Loki claimed that Freyja had been the mistress of all the gods, even her own brother. He even boasted that he had seduced Thór's wife, Sif, and Njörð's wife, Skaði—even though Skaði had known that he had been responsible for her father's death. At the end of the dinner, Thór returned and drove Loki out with his hammer, and the hail of accusations was cut short. This was the last dinner of the gods which Loki attended, and during its course it became clear that the gods knew perfectly well that Loki was to be their arch-enemy.

Retaliatory references were made to Loki's own unnatural sexual practices. Loki had three monstrous offspring by the giantess Angrboða (Distress-Bringer): the wolf Fenrir, the World Serpent, and the ruler of the Otherworld, Hel. Óðin refers to him at the dinner as 'the father of the wolf', but Loki was also the parent (the mother, in fact), of Óðin's marvellous flying horse, Sleipnir, which had eight legs.

The story of Sleipnir's birth is given by Snorri in *Gylfaginning*. When the gods had established Miðgarð

Dragons of the North.
Above: The masterly dragon-head on one of the wooden
posts found amongst the furniture of the Oseberg ship.
The artist was nicknamed the 'Academician' by the scholar
Shetelig because of the conservative elegance and precision
of his work. The marvellous intricacy of whorls and coils
on the neck below the snarling mask makes this his
masterpiece.
Below: A gilt-bronze winged dragon from Sweden, dating
from the eighth century

threatened him with death unless he came up with a way of breaking the contract. To save his skin, Loki accordingly swore to do the builder out of his agreed payment, by whatever means. That same evening, when the builder and his stallion were carting stones, a mare came galloping out of the forest and whinnied at the stallion. The stallion broke free from his traces and ran off in pursuit of the mare. With the stallion missing, there was no chance of finishing the work in time. The builder, enraged, revealed himself as a Rock Giant in disguise, whereupon Thór killed him with his Hammer. Soon afterwards, Loki (the mare had been Loki in disguise) gave birth to a grey foal with eight legs—Sleipnir.

The presence of Loki in the Norse pantheon allowed the poets and myth-makers a vehicle for abusing the gods, or laughing at them, which argues a more wholesome respect for them than an attitude of craven servility. It was, if anything, a Homeric attitude. But there was no jesting about the culmination of Loki's treachery in Ásgarð. It was Loki who precipitated the final horror of Ragnarök by his part in the slaying of the White God, Óðin's favourite son, Baldur. For this crime, Loki was seized by the gods, bound with the entrails of his own son and fettered deep inside an underground cavern, while serpents fastened to the roof dripped venom onto his face. His faithful wife, Sigyn, crouched beside him, catching the venom in a bowl, but whenever she had to turn aside to empty the bowl, the venom splashed on his face, and Loki would writhe in such paroxysms of anguish that the earth would quake and volcanoes would belch fire. At Ragnarök, however, Loki would break free, and steer the ship carrying the sons of Múspell, the demons of destruction, from the east. During the battle, he and Heimdall would kill one another.

Snorri wrote of Baldur in *Gylfaginning*: [He] is pre-eminent, and everyone praises him. He is so beautiful and bright that he glows with radiance, and one plant is so white that it is likened to Baldur's brow [the ox-eye daisy]; it is the whitest of all plants, and from it you can remark his beauty both of hair and body. He is the wisest of the gods and the fairest spoken and the most gracious, but such is his nature that his judgement never holds. His home is Breiðablik [Broad Splendour], which is in the sky, and nothing unclean is allowed there.'

Baldur was the beloved of the gods. But he dreamed that his life was threatened, and so his father, Óðin, descended to the Otherworld and forced a dead sibyl to come to life and tell him the future. He was told that Baldur would be killed, and this would lead to Ragnarök. Meanwhile, the other gods resolved that oaths should be demanded of all objects to spare Baldur. His mother, Frigg, collected pledges from fire, water, all metals, stones, the earth, trees, all sicknesses, all poisons, beasts, birds and serpents, that they would never harm Baldur. Since Baldur was now impervious to wounds,

and Ásgarð, a builder arrived and offered to build a great wall for Ásgarð that would be secure against the giants. The terms he offered were these: that if he completed the work in one winter, he would be rewarded with the goddess Freyja, and the sun and the moon. The gods eventually agreed, at Loki's prompting, on condition that he did all the work unaided, and that if the work were not completed by the first day of summer, he would not get paid. The builder asked only that he should be allowed to use his stallion, Svaðilfari (Hazard-Farer), and Loki strongly urged that this should be accepted. The builder began work on the first day of winter and the gods were astonished to see the huge blocks of stone the stallion could drag. With only three days left before the end of winter the work had progressed so well that only the gate was left to be put in place, and now the gods became alarmed. They blamed Loki bitterly for making this disastrous bargain, and

he used to entertain the gods by letting them shoot arrows at him, strike at him with swords or pelt him with stones, knowing that nothing would hurt him.

But there was one living organism from which Frigg had not bothered to exact the oath: a slender shoot called mistletoe which grew not from the ground but on a tree, the oak. She had thought it too young and feeble to matter. Loki, consumed with spite against the popular Baldur, disguised himself as an old woman and wormed this information out of Frigg. He then conceived his plan. One of the gods, Óðin's son Höð, was blind, and could take no part in this sport of pelting Baldur for fun. So Loki cut a sprig of mistletoe in the shape of a javelin and took it to Höð, who was very strong, and invited him to join in the play; he put the missile in Höð's hand, and directed his aim. The shaft of mistletoe pierced Baldur's body, and Baldur fell dead to the ground.

This was the greatest tragedy that had ever befallen gods or men. The gods were struck dumb with horror. No vengeance could be taken on the spot, for it was such a holy place. When they tried to speak they could only weep, but Óðin had the bitterest grief to bear, for he knew better than the others what a disaster the death of Baldur was.

When the gods recovered their senses, Frigg promised her love and undying gratitude to anyone who would undertake to ride down to Hel and offer a ransom for the release of Baldur. It was another of Óðin's sons, Hermóð the Valiant, who volunteered; he mounted Óðin's horse, Sleipnir, and galloped away.

Meanwhile the gods took Baldur's body down to the seashore, planning to launch Baldur's great ship, Hringhorni, as a funeral pyre. But the ship was too heavy for the gods to move, so they sent word to Giantland for the giantess, Hyrrokin, who came riding on a wolf, using a serpent for reins. At the first heave she launched the ship: flames shot from the rollers, and all the world trembled.

When Baldur's body was carried on board, his wife, Nanna, died of grief and was laid on the pyre beside him. Thór hallowed the pyre with his hammer. All the gods attended: Óðin with Frigg, his Valkyries and his ravens; Frey in his chariot drawn by the golden boar; Heimdall on his horse Golden-Forelock; Freyja in her chariot pulled by cats, and a great host of Frost Giants and Rock Giants. Óðin laid on the pyre his gold arm-ring, Draupnir, from which eight rings of similar weight dripped every ninth night. Baldur's horse, too, was led to the pyre in all its harness.

Meanwhile, Hermóð rode Sleipnir for nine nights and days through deep, dark dales down the perilous road to the Otherworld until he reached the bridge that resounded only under the feet of the living. The maiden who guarded it told him that netherward and northward lay the way to Hel. Hermóð rode on until he

Above: A small silver pendant from Birka in Sweden, one of a pair. It is tempting to associate the rider with Baldur, the White God

Far left: The 'Bound Devil' on a cross at Kirkby Stephen in Cumbria, England, dating from the Viking period when there was substantial Scandinavian settlement in the North of England. He is usually interpreted as the horned Loki lying fettered in a cavern after contriving Baldur's death, while serpents fastened to the roof drip venom on his face

reached the Gates of Hel, which Sleipnir cleared in one mighty leap. Then he rode to the Hall of Hel, where he dismounted; when he entered, he found his brother Baldur seated on a throne of honour.

Next morning, Hermóð told Hel of the grief of the gods, and asked her to allow Baldur to ride back with him to Ásgarð. But Hel wanted to make sure that Baldur was as well-loved as everyone claimed. She would only release Baldur, she said, if all things in the world, both animate and inanimate, would weep for him—but if anyone refused, then Baldur must stay.

When Hermóð returned to Ásgarð with the news, the gods sent messengers to every corner of the world to ask all things to 'weep Baldur back from Hel'. Everyone and everything did so, both men and beasts, earth and stones and trees and metals.

On their way home, thinking that their errand was complete, the messengers came across an old witch crouching in a cave who called herself Thökk. They asked her to weep for Baldur, but she replied:

> Thökk will weep
> Dry tears
> For the funeral of Baldur;
> Alive or dead
> I loved not the Old One's son.
> Let Hel keep what she has.

Everyone knew that the old witch must have been none other than Loki, who had wrought so much mischief amongst the gods.

Now Ragnarök was at hand. Loki had been caught and bound, but now broke free. The universe was consumed in a holocaust of destruction. But after Ragnarök, Baldur returned from the dead to a new and revitalized heaven:

> Unsown fields
> Will grow rich with corn,
> All ills will get better,
> Baldur will come.

The story of his death is the only myth about Baldur recounted by Snorri Sturluson. In it, Baldur appears as the perfect, innocent martyr, a portrait with definite Christian overtones.

There are faint echoes in ancient place-names of a cult of Baldur, which was presumably a fertility/warrior cult. But, as with Loki, Baldur's significance in the Norse pantheon of the Viking Age lay not in his relationship with mankind, but as a catalyst in the myths surrounding Ragnarök, the end of the world.

Right: This magnificent three-ringed gold collar from Gotland, with its startling use of miniature masks, represents the best of Migration Period craftsmanship

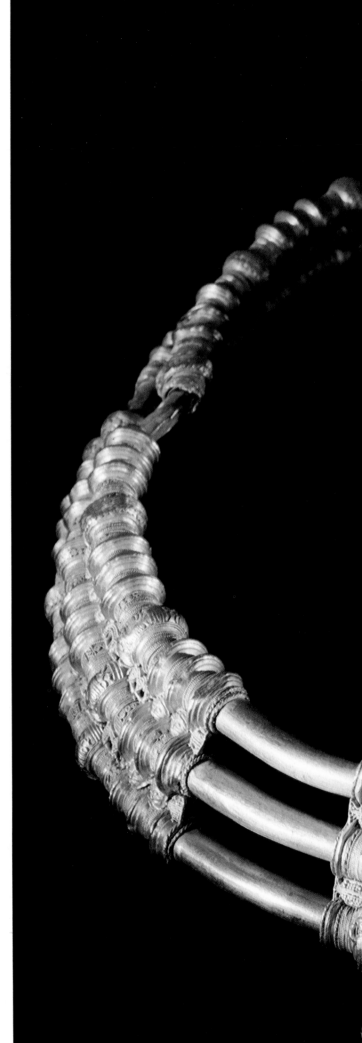

CHOOSERS OF THE SLAIN

VALKYRIES AND THE SPIRITS OF THE OTHERWORLD

Apart from the gods of Ásgarð, the Æsir and the Vanir, there were various groups of lesser deities and spirits, all of whom played a part in the affairs of mankind although not all of them were venerated or formally worshipped. They included trolls, dwarves, elves, minor goddesses and land-spirits.

There were three groups of goddesses whose functions often seemed to overlap: the Norns, the Valkyries, and the *dísir*. The most ancient of these were the Norns, who represented the powers of destiny to which both men and gods, even Óðin himself, were subject. They are met first tending the Well of Fate at the roots of the World Tree, Yggdrasil: three old crones of immense and implacable power, akin to the Greek *Moirai*, named

Left: The misty mountainscapes of Iceland, where lava has congealed into fantastic shapes and the emptiness is eerie, were easily peopled with trolls and spirits

but impersonal. Their names were Urðr, Verðandi, and Skuld. Urðr is the same word as Anglo-Saxon *Wyrd*, meaning Fate, which still survives in the Scottish phrase 'to dree one's weird', meaning 'to endure one's fate'. Thus, the names of the three Norns can be translated as Fate, Being, and Necessity; or more loosely, Past, Present and Future. In *The Sibyl's Prophecy* it is three monstrous women who cast the first shadow over the Golden Age of Ásgarð:

> They played chess on the grass
> With gladsome hearts,
> They never had any
> Lack of gold;
> Until there came
> Three giant maidens,
> Awful in might,
> From Giantland.

If these three mighty maidens, born of giants, were the Norns, they must stand as symbols of Time, which corrupts the timeless existence of the youthful gods and compromises their immortality. Time and destiny were inexorable powers before which even the gods had to bow.

The Valkyries, Choosers of the Slain, were represented somewhat romantically in later myths, as the warrior handmaidens of Óðin, but originally they were demons of carnage and death who devoured corpses on the battlefield, like wolves. In this they resembled the Greek Furies with their thirst for retribution and bloody revenge. This was reflected in their names, which included Hlökk (Shrieking), Göll (Screaming), and Skögul (Raging).

After the Viking defeat at the Battle of Clontarf in Ireland in 1014, a Norse poet portrayed them in their primitive form, exulting in blood and weaving the web

of war. The description is preserved in the thirteenth-century Icelandic masterpiece, *Njál's Saga*:

Blood rains
From the cloudy web
On the broad loom of slaughter.
The web of man,
Grey as armour,
Is now being woven;
The Valkyries
Will cross it
With a crimson weft.

The warp is made
Of human entrails;
Human heads
Are used as weights;
The heddle-rods
Are blood-wet spears;
The shafts are iron-bound,
And arrows are the shuttles.
With swords we will weave
This web of battle. . . .

It is terrible now
To look around,
As a blood-red cloud
Darkens the sky.
The heavens are stained
With the blood of men,
As the Valkyries
Sing their song. . . .

Let us ride our horses
Hard on bare backs,
With swords unsheathed,
Away from here.

Choosers of the slain: the Valkyries were originally demons of carnage who in later myths became the warrior handmaidens of Óðin, selecting champions for Valhöll and tending to their needs there.
Far left: A Valkyrie welcomes a mounted warrior to Valhöll with a horn of ale in a detail from a Gotland picture-stone, dating from the eighth century.
Above left: A 'horn of plenty' found in a Viking grave, containing the most precious belongings of the dead man.
Above: Sixth-century silver-gilt pendant found in a grave in Sweden, representing a Valkyrie offering a horn

These harpies are far removed from the almost gracious ladies in full armour who escorted Óðin's fallen champions from the battlefield and welcomed them to Valhöll with horns of mead. They are even further from the still more romanticized figures who play such a part in the exploits of legendary Germanic heroes. The most celebrated of these Valkyries was Brynhild, the heroine of the story of Sigurð the Volsung (Siegfried in the German *Nibelungenlied* which Wagner used as the basis for *The Ring of the Nibelung*). Here, history and legend have become hopelessly enmeshed. Brynhild and Sigurð are presumed to be the fictionalized versions of a historical pair, the Frankish king Sigebert (murdered in AD 575) and his Visigothic wife from Spain, Queen Brunhilda (died AD 613).

In the legend, Brynhild appears in a double role, both as a supernatural Valkyrie and as a human princess. In one of the poems of the Edda she is known as Sigrdrífa (Victory-Giver), a Valkyrie who had incurred the wrath of Óðin by awarding victory in battle to the wrong king. For her disobedience she was plunged into an enchanted sleep within a wall of fire. None but the greatest hero in the world could penetrate the fire to waken her, and the man who did so was the peerless Sigurð of the Volsungs. (We return to the story of Sigurð and Brynhild in the final chapter.)

In their supernatural guise, the Valkyries were envisaged as guardian spirits, *fylgjur* (fetches), who supported and encouraged chosen champions and their families. But this function was more in the province of the third group of female spirits, the *dísir* or 'goddesses'. Snorri Sturluson associated them with Freyja, the great *dís,* as having power over the forces of natural increase. From other sources it becomes clear that they were also thought of as tutelary goddesses attached to a particular family or clan. Unlike the Norns and the Valkyries, the dísir were cult-figures who were worshipped in both public and private ceremonies, particularly in Sweden. A festival called the *dísablót* (sacrifice to the dísir) was held in their honour at the beginning of winter. They are depicted visiting houses to bring good luck and bestow blessings on new-born children, rather like the fairy-godmothers of folklore. The dísir were thought of as being basically well-disposed towards mankind, but they could also be merciless. In the saga literature of Iceland there are several references to a young man called Thiðrandi 'whom the dísir slew'. Thiðrandi was the son of a man called Hall of Síða, who was one of the first Icelandic chieftains to be converted to Christianity shortly before the year 1000. *The Tale of Thiðrandi and Thórhall* gives a graphic account of the manner of his death. His father, Hall of Síða, was holding an autumn feast, possibly a dísablót. That night, when all the guests had gone to bed, there was a loud knocking at the door. Young Thiðrandi rose and went to the door, carrying his sword. There was no one there, but Thiðrandi went outside to have a look around. He heard the sound of horses galloping from the north, and at first assumed that they were late arrivals coming to the feast, but then he saw nine women, all dressed in black and brandishing drawn swords. He also heard riders coming from the south; this was another group of nine women, but these were dressed in shining raiment and riding white horses. Thiðrandi tried to get back to the house, but the black-clad woman cut him off. Thiðrandi defended himself valiantly, but before the white-clad women could come to his aid, he had been dealt a mortal wound. Before he died, he told the story of what had happened, and his father's friend, Thórhall the Prophet, interpreted the events. He explained that the black-clad women had been dísir, the attendant spirits of the family, who had known that Hall of Síða and all his family, and soon the whole of Iceland, would embrace the new religion. They had now taken their final sacrificial tribute from the family. The white-clad dísir were spirits of the new faith who were not yet powerful enough in a still-pagan land to prevent the death of their favourite.

Of the more earthly spirits, the giants of the creation myths, who lived in Giantland, were a malevolent race, implacably hostile to the gods and to men. But they were also widely believed to inhabit mountains and caves, and were called trolls. In Iceland, where grotesque volcanic formations are easy to identify with monstrous shapes, they were frequently linked with prominent features in the landscape. Although most trolls were thought to be malignant and stupid, easily tricked by the nimble-witted, some became almost deified as benign guardian spirits, like Bárð of Snæfellsness, in Iceland, of whom many entertaining tales were told. In Norway, the mountain of Dovrefell was regarded as the home of a giant called Dofri, who was considered to be a tutelary spirit, almost a foster father, to King Harald

Fine-Hair, the vigorous despot who, during the ninth century, united Norway under one crown for the first time.

In the creation myths, the dwarves came into being as maggots infesting the body of the primeval giant Ýmir. They were the quintessential craftsmen of the world, makers of all the major treasures of Norse mythology and the repositories of secret wisdom. They lived in rocks or underground, and if they could be enticed out into the sunlight, they were turned to stone. There is no evidence that dwarves were ever venerated, but men were certainly wary of them and admired their skills. Care was taken not to offend them or steal from them, for such possessions were usually cursed.

Another race of earth spirits, the elves, suffered a certain erosion of their importance and authority as the centuries passed. In the creation myths, they are frequently coupled with the gods themselves, but one rung lower in the hierarchy. Snorri Sturluson, alone of the sources, differentiated between Light Elves and Dark Elves. The Light Elves, more beautiful than the sun, lived in a splendid place called Álfheim (Elfworld) that bordered on Ásgarð, while the Dark Elves, black as pitch, lived underground. In *The Sibyl's Prophecy*, the elves shared with the gods the horror of Ragnarök: 'How fare the gods? How fare the elves?' is the refrain that tolls through the fabric of the poem.

Because they lived in mounds, elves were frequently associated in folklore with the dead. A ninth-century Norwegian king called Olaf, reputed to be the uncle of Harald Fine-Hair, was nicknamed the 'Elf of Geirstadir' after men started making sacrifice to his burial mound in times of famine and pestilence. There is one recorded instance in the Icelandic sagas, in *Kormák's Saga,* of a man in Iceland making sacrifice to the elves: he had been wounded in a duel, and was healed after slaughtering an ox before a hillock inhabited by elves, smearing the hillock with the blood and leaving the meat as an offering. In later folklore, they had become a small, homely people, friendly to man for the most part, possessed of certain magical powers but nevertheless dangerous to cross. They could cohabit with humans, but the outcome was usually tragic.

Finally there were the *landvættir* (land-spirits). They were thought of as powers, usually invisible, who resided in the land itself and were responsible for its welfare. They had to be treated with a great deal of respect. In the first pagan Icelandic law-code, introduced when the Icelandic Parliament first met in 930, the initial clause stipulated that no one might approach the country in ships furnished with dragon-heads ('gaping heads and yawning snouts'). If ships were so furnished, the dragon-heads had to be removed before land was sighted, lest the land-spirits take fright.

The early Viking settlers of Iceland took particular care not to affront the land-spirits of the empty land they planned to occupy. The first settler, Ingólf Arnarson, cast overboard within sight of land the sacred carved pillars of his ancestral high-seat in Norway (carved with images of the gods), and vowed to make his home wherever they might be washed ashore. In effect, he was sending the pillars ahead as ambassadors to the land-spirits, confident that they would guide the pillars to a place which was acceptable to them. His example was followed by many of the settlers who came after him.

Snorri Sturluson, in his monumental *Heimskringla* (*History of the Kings of Norway*) records a delightful story about the land-spirits of Iceland and how they saved the country from invasion. It seems that King Harald Gormsson of Denmark was stung by some affront to his royal authority into planning to invade Iceland late in the tenth century. As part of his planning he hired a wizard to reconnoitre the country. The wizard swam to Iceland in the form of a whale, and noted that the mountains and hills were swarming with land-spirits. In the first fjord he visited, he was met by a great dragon, flanked by a host of lesser crawling monsters, who spewed poison on him. In the second fjord an enormous eagle whose wing-tips brushed the mountains on either side swooped down on him, attended by great flocks of other birds. In the third fjord a gigantic bull came wading out to sea towards him, bellowing hideously. In the fourth fjord he encountered a huge Rock Giant carrying an iron staff, with a legion of other giants in support. At that, the wizard gave up and returned to Norway, where he advised King Harald to call off the invasion. These four symbols, the giant, the eagle, the bull and the dragon, now appear on the Icelandic Coat of Arms.

Although less spectacular than the gods of Ásgarð, the various spirits and minor goddesses survived the advent of Christianity much more stubbornly than the higher deities. In the oldest church laws of the Scandinavian countries there was much greater emphasis placed on the banning of belief in land-spirits than on eradicating faith in pagan gods. In the later Middle Ages it was still common for women to place food as an offering before cairns, caves or hillocks to appease the land-spirits. Even to this day, there are country folk who prefer to play safe with the unseen powers.

The dwarves were the legendary craftsmen of Viking Scandinavia; most of the fabled treasures were said to have been fashioned by them.
Right: A square-headed brooch from Jämtland in Sweden, dating from the Migration Period; this was the sort of elaborate ornamentation which the Viking myths associated with the dwarves.
Inset: A dwarf-figure at work at his forge depicted in a detail from the side of a twelfth-century baptismal font from Gotland

the way to hel

death and the after-life

In Norse mythology, Hel is the name of both the Otherworld itself and the hideous goddess who is its ruler, the Queen of the Dead. In the creation myths, there is mention of an even more remote Otherworld, called either Niflhel or Niflheim (Misty Hell or Misty World), and this region of ultimate negation had existed even before the creation of the world. It was the northern region of Ginnungagap, the Great Void. There are indications in the poems of the Edda that there were degrees of Hel, and that Niflhel was, literally, the end:

> To nine worlds I came,
> To Niflhel beneath
> Where the dead from Hel descend.

Left: The stark upright stones that mark out a Viking burial-plot in the form of a ship; from Blomsholm, in Bohuslän

There is no single, clear picture of Hel itself in the sources: it is an amorphous region of mighty spaces and barriers, an immensity of darkness and cold. The road to Hel, the Helway, led netherwards and northwards, a long and perilous journey which the dead had to trudge over mountains and through forests and deep, dark valleys. The mouth of the road seems to have been a black cave guarded by a fearsome hound called Garm with a blood-smeared chest. Near the end of the Helway flowed a boundary river, Gjöll (Howling) which had to be crossed by the Gjöll Bridge. The bridge was roofed with burning gold and guarded by a mysterious maiden. Farther on stood the portals of the Otherworld, Hel Gates; behind them lay the Hall of Death, where Hel herself ruled supreme.

If the region of Hel is not envisaged with any great clarity in the sources, Snorri Sturluson has left us a stark portrait of Hel herself. Along with the wolf Fenrir and the World Serpent, Hel was one of the monstrous off-spring of Loki and the giantess Angrboða (Distress-Bringer). According to Snorri she looked like a rotting corpse, half black and half flesh-coloured: 'In Niflheim she has a mighty dwelling, with walls exceedingly high and huge portals. Her palace is called Sleetcold, her platter is Hunger, her knife is Famine; her slave is called Senility, her bondmaid Dotage; her threshold is Pitfall, her pallet Bedridden, her bed-curtains Woeful Wan.'

As the Odinic cult grew in strength, a distinction emerged between the worthy dead who were warriors killed on the battlefield and were sent to Valhöll as Óðin's chosen host, and the unworthy dead who died in their beds and were consigned to Hel. Come Ragnarök, Óðin's champions would fight on the side of the gods, but the dead of Hel would fight against them. There is also a hint of Hel containing a special place of punishment for the wicked, particularly those who had committed the two sins most abhorrent to the Nordic code of conduct, oath-breaking and murder (secret killing). As *The Sibyl's Prophecy* puts it:

> A hall she saw stand
> Far from the sun,
> Its doors facing north,
> On Corpse Strand.
> Drops of poison
> Dripped through the smoke-hole;
> The hall is wattled
> With serpents' backs.
>
> She saw there wading
> Through turbulent waters
> Men forsworn,
> And murderers,
> And those who take
> The wives of others.

This purgatorial aspect of Hel is often presumed to show the influence of Christianity on Viking thinking, and this may well be so. The original concept of Hel seems closely bound up with the etymological meaning of the word as 'a place of concealment', in other words: the grave.

There was no consistency in the way that the Norse-men viewed death, the grave and the prospects of an after-life. For the most part, it was believed that life went on in one form or another after death and that there was continuing contact between the living and the dead, but the precise nature of that life after death was expressed in many different ways. To simplify the position, the various views might be grouped under two main headings: the idea that the dead lived on in the grave itself, and the idea that the dead went on a journey from the grave.

The latter concept was explicitly expressed in the mythology of Ásgarð and was symbolized by the visit of Hermóð the Valiant to Hel, seeking the release of Baldur, and a journey made by Óðin himself in search of knowledge of the future. Even mounted on a super-natural flying steed like Sleipnir, the journey took nine days and nights. For the dead it would take much longer, unless they were lucky enough to be given a ride by the Valkyries as one of Óðin's chosen *élite* bound for Valhöll.

The dead were laid in their grave-mounds with a supply of food and all manner of useful or decorative equipment: weapons, personal possessions, ornaments, treasure, even farm implements. This practice was meant both to help the dead on their journey to the Otherworld, and to allow them to keep up appearances there. No doubt there was also an element of impressing the neighbours in this world, too, by a display of con-spicuous wealth at the funeral. Similarly, the practice of burying a horse or horses with the dead, and even dogs,

may have had a double purpose, symbolizing a dedication or sacrifice to the gods as well as providing transport and company on the way to Hel.

In one of the thirteenth-century Icelandic sagas, *Gisli's Saga*, there is a description of the funeral of Véstein, the victim of a murder, in which special shoes called Hel-shoes were tied on to the dead man's feet for the long march to the Otherworld. This is the only written reference to Hel-shoes that has survived, and it appears to have survived only because of the peculiar circumstances of the funeral. The man who tied on the Hel-shoes, Thorgrím, had been Véstein's secret murderer, and when Thorgrím in turn was murdered in revenge by the hero of the saga, Gísli Súrsson, the gesture with the Hel-shoes was remembered and matched by Gísli at Thorgrím's boat-burial. At Véstein's funeral, the murderer had said, 'If these come loose, then I don't know how to fasten Hel-shoes.'

The picture-stones of Gotland, mostly dating from the early Viking Age, are rich in motifs showing slain warriors going to Valhöll to join Óðin's élite army of champions.
Below: A picture-stone from Larbrö, Gotland, portrays a dead warrior on the back of Óðin's eight-legged steed, Sleipnir. Behind it are three men with their swords pointing downwards, signifying death. In the lower panel, a mounted warrior followed by four others on foot is greeted at the doors of Valhöll by a figure holding a horn.
Below left: Valhöll itself is usually depicted on the picture-stones as a hutch-like structure; in the literary sources, however, it had 940 doorways, through each of which nearly a thousand warriors could march shoulder to shoulder. Their days were spent in gaming and fighting, and their nights in feasting and drinking

At Thorgrím's funeral, Gísli placed a huge boulder into the boat to moor it in the grave, and said: 'If this breaks loose, then I don't know how to secure a boat.'

There is an apparent contradiction here in the idea of mooring a boat in a grave, when presumably the boat reflected a more ancient notion of a voyage to the Otherworld. But it is not unique: the magnificent Oseberg Ship, which was excavated from a burial mound in Norway in 1904 and is presumed to be the grave of a ninth-century Norwegian queen, had been moored by a cable round a huge boulder in the mound. The Oseberg ship is only one of hundreds of boat-burials that have been unearthed in Scandinavia (five have been found in Iceland, to corroborate the scattered references in the sagas). Some of the boats had been laid upside down, others were simply suggested symbolically by stones arranged round the grave. The idea of a voyage, so strikingly illustrated in the funeral of Baldur,

has been superseded in such cases by less explicit concepts of the ship as an adjunct of death and perhaps even a symbol of rebirth. The evidence of archaeology seldom fits the literary picture exactly.

The literary sources also imply that the dead might need human company. The Icelandic *Landnámabók* (*Book of Settlements*) records that one of the early settlers, Ásmund Atlason, was given a boat-burial, and that his slave was buried with him. Some time later, Ásmund's voice was heard chanting a verse in the mound, the gist of which was that he objected to the slave's company and would rather be on his own. After that the mound was opened up and the body of the slave removed, and Ásmund relapsed into a contented silence.

The Arab traveller Ibn Rustah, who visited the Scandinavian settlements along the Volga in the first half of the tenth century, wrote: 'When one of their chieftains dies, they dig a grave like a big house and put

him inside it. With him they put his clothes and the gold bracelets he wore and also much food and drinking vessels and coins. They also put his favourite wife in the grave with him, while she is still living; thereafter the entrance to the cairn is blocked, and she dies there.'

Human sacrifices to accompany the dead have been identified at several archaeological sites. The queen buried in the Oseberg ship had a young slave-girl with her, and other examples have been found in Sweden and on the Isle of Man. Another Arab traveller in Russia, Ibn Fadlan, witnessed a Viking funeral on the Volga in 922 and left a vivid description of the rites that took place (translation by the late S. M. Stern and R. Pinder-Wilson):

'I was told that when their chieftains died one of the last things which was done was cremation . . . When a chief died his family asks his slave women and slaves, "Who will die with him?" Then one of them

The four-wheeled cart found in the Oseberg ship-burial is elaborately carved and is full of echoes of Viking mythology and legends. It seems to have been used for ceremonial purposes—perhaps for the transport of images of the gods.

Above, far left: The body of the cart rested on separate, curved pieces of wood that served as a cradle; they terminated in fierce human masks.

Above left: On one side of the cart is this scene of a woman with streaming hair, apparently restraining a man's sword-arm as he strikes at a rider accompanied by a dog. Below is a frieze of coiled serpents and gripping-beasts.

Above, top: A man grappling with serpents, from one of four sledges which accompanied the cart.

Above: The scenes on the front and back boards of the cart reflect those on the sledges. They show a wild confusion of snakes and animals attacking a single man. This motif is usually associated with the death of Gunnar in the snake-pit

says, "I will". When she has said this there is no backing out . . . most of those who agree are women slaves . . .

'[When, as in this case, a girl had volunteered] two female slaves were appointed to guard her wherever she went so that they even washed her feet with their own hands. Then they began to get things ready for the dead man; to cut out his clothes and do all that should be done, but the slave drank and sang every day happily and joyfully.

'When the day came that the dead man should be burned together with his slave, I went to the river where the ship lay. It had been hauled up on land and supported by four posts of birch and other wood. Around it was arranged what looked like a large pile of wood . . . The corpse still lay in the grave from which they had not yet taken it. They then brought a bier which was placed in the ship, they covered it with Byzantine brocaded tapestries and with cushions of Byzantine brocade.

'Then an old woman, whom they call the Angel of Death, came and spread these hangings on the bier. She is in charge of embalming the dead man and preparing him and it is she who kills the girl. The one I saw was a strongly built and grim figure. When they came to the grave they removed the earth . . . The corpse did not smell at all and nothing but the colour of his flesh had changed. They then clothed him in drawers and trousers, boots and tunic, and a brocade mantle with gold buttons on it. They placed a cap made of brocade and sable on his head. They carried him into a tent which stood on the ship, and laid him on the tapestry and propped him up with the cushions. Then they brought *nabidh* [a fermented drink], fruit and sweet-smelling herbs and laid these beside him. Next they brought bread, meat and onions and threw these beside him. Next they took two horses which they caused to run until they were sweating, after which they cut them in pieces with a sword and threw their flesh into the ship. Then they brought two cows, which they also cut into pieces and threw them in. The slave woman who wished to be killed went to and fro from one tent to another, and the man of each tent had intercourse with her and said, "Tell your master that I have done this out of love for him."

'It was now Friday afternoon and they took the slave away to something which looked like the frame of a door. Then she put her legs on the hands of the men and was thus lifted, so that she was above the top of the door-frame, and she said something [this was done three times] . . . Then they gave her a chicken and she cut off its head and threw it away. Then they took the hen and threw it into the ship. Then I asked what she had done and my interpreter answered: "The first time they lifted her up she said, 'Look, I see my mother and father'; the second time she said, 'Look, I see all my dead relations sitting together'; the third time she said, 'Look, I see my master sitting in paradise and paradise is beautiful and green, and together with him are men and young boys. He called to me, so let me go to him.'" They then took her to the ship. She then took off two arm-bands which she had on and gave them to the old woman who was called the Angel of Death, who was the one who would kill her; she also took off two ankle-rings which she wore and gave them to the two girls who were in attendance on her and who are the daughters of the woman called the Angel of Death. Then they took her to the ship, but did not allow her to enter the tent. Then came men who had shields and staves, and gave her a beaker of *nabidh*. She sang over it and drained it. The interpreter said to me, "She now takes farewell of her friends." Then she was given another beaker. She took this and sang for a long time, but the old woman warned her that she should drink quickly and go into the tent where her master lay. When I looked at her, she seemed bemused, she wanted to go into the tent and put her head between it and the ship, then the old woman took her hand and made her enter the tent and went in with her. The men began to beat with their staves on the shields so that her shrieks should not be heard and the other girls should not be frightened and thus not seek death with their masters. Then six men went into the tent and all had intercourse with the girl; then they laid her by the side of her dead master, then two took her legs, two took her hands, and the old woman who is called the Angel of Death put a rope round her neck, with the ends in opposite directions, and gave it to two men to pull; then she came with a dagger with a broad blade and began to thrust it time and again between the girl's ribs, while the two men choked her with the rope so that she died.

'Then came one who was nearest related to the dead man. He took a piece of wood and fired it. Then he went backwards towards the ship with his face towards the people and held the torch in one hand, his other hand was on his backside. He was naked. Thus the wood which lay under the ship was fired after they had laid the slave woman whom they had killed by the side of her master. [One of the men said to me], "You Arabs are stupid." "Why?" I asked and he answered: "Well, because you take those you love and honour most and put them in the earth and the worms and earth devour them. We burn them in the blinking of an eyelid so that [they go] to paradise at that very moment."'

The funeral rites described so vividly by Ibn Fadlan contain many elements, such as the Angel of Death, which are not found in Norse sources. The decapitation of the chicken, on the other hand, is a tantalizing echo

Right: Enigmatic figure from the side of a ninth-century bowl found in a burial mound in western Norway. The bowl contained the bosses of shields probably left in the embers when a ship was burnt on the spot. The figure is typically Celtic in style and was probably made in Ireland

of a visit by the hero Hadding to the Otherworld, where his supernatural female guide cut off the head of a cock and threw it over the boundary wall of Hel. The Scandinavians in Russia may have been influenced by foreign customs by this time, but there remain unmistakable parallels with the Odinic cult rituals reflected in the Norse literary sources, especially the ceremonial sacrifice of the girl by simultaneous strangling and stabbing.

The Norse chieftain on the Volga was assumed to go to Paradise 'in the twinkling of an eyelid'. Some chieftains found paradise right on their doorstep; they were believed to live on with their departed kin inside sacred mountains, enjoying a kind of private family Valhöll of their own. The most interesting example of this occurs in the thirteenth-century Icelandic *Eyrbyggja Saga*, whose author took a keen antiquarian interest in the old pagan rites. When Thorstein Cod-Biter, who was the son of a first settler and a fervent adherent of Thór,

drowned at sea in the year 938, his shepherd saw an extraordinary sight when he looked towards Helgafell: 'He saw the whole north side of the mountain standing open, and inside it he could see great fires burning, and he could hear the noise of feasting and clamour over the ale-horns. And as he strained to make out what was being said, he could hear that Thorstein Cod-Biter and his crew were being welcomed into the mountain, and that Thorstein was being invited to sit in the place of honour opposite his father.'

The idea that members of certain families 'died into a mountain' does not occur often in the sources, and is probably a late development. In the Icelandic sagas, stories of the dead tended to be more earthy and peasant in character. When someone died, the first act was to close the nostrils and mouth, and sometimes the eyes. But even in this tradition, death did not necessarily mean the extinction of all life. The dead man lived on in the

grave, like Gunnar of Hlíðarendi in *Njál's Saga*, who chanted a verse in his burial mound. The dead could, and frequently did, continue to exercise influence on the living, long after they were buried. One of the villains in *Laxdæla Saga*, Killer-Hrapp, asked to be buried upright under the threshold of his house, so that he could keep an even better watch over his household, which he proceeded to do with a vengeance. 'And difficult as he had been to deal with during his life, he was now very much worse after death, for his corpse would not rest in its grave; people say he murdered most of his servants in his hauntings after death, and caused grievous harm to most of his neighbours.' Physical violence was a commonplace amongst these living dead who rose from their graves to terrorize the living, and many a hero in the sagas made his name by the manner in which he fought and dealt with them. Great care had to be taken with the corpse of a man who might prove

difficult after death; sometimes a hole would be broken in the wall of the house through which the corpse would be taken out, to prevent him finding his way back into the house through the door. Death merely increased the brute strength and malevolence of these dead-walkers; often they had to be exhumed and reburied elsewhere, or even cremated, before their ghosts were finally laid to rest. Even then, their malign influence could linger on for generations, blighting the land they had haunted and the families who farmed it.

Such stories belong more to the realm of folklore than mythology. They have none of the elegiac magnificence of Ásgarð or the aristocratic sophistication of the cult of Óðin, but they have their own robust validity, the blunt response of peasants who might venerate Thór and Frey as gods but who mostly relied on their own burly strength to cope with the mysteries of nature and the eerie power of the elements.

Burial treasure of the Vikings. In their graves they were surrounded by their choicest personal possessions, as well as by the more utilitarian objects they would require for the journey to the Otherworld. A dead Viking wanted to be able to cut a good figure in the next world.
Far left: Gilt-bronze bridle-mount from a rich Swedish grave in Gotland, dating from the ninth century. This is one of a number of superbly decorated pieces. The familiar 'gripping-beast' has his paws in small, round apertures.
Left: Beautifully worked gold brooches from Hornelund, in Denmark, dating from the tenth century.
Above: Silver ring from Hornelund in Denmark, dating from the tenth century—sinuous Viking craftsmanship at its best

103

sacred stones

norsemen at worship

After so many centuries, it has become practically‹ impossible to know what the Norsemen actually *felt* about their gods. Archaeology and literary sources can tell us a lot about the kind of concepts that were prevalent in the Viking Age, but questions still arise. What was the relationship between a man and his gods? Between man and priest? Between priest and temple? In a pantheistic religion that tended to be flexible and individualistic, can we ever get inside the minds of men at worship, separated as we are from them by so many conditioned centuries of Christian thinking? There is little evidence of fanaticism of belief, but does this necessarily mean that there was little fervour? Could a

Left: The three great royal burial mounds at Old Uppsala, a major centre of pagan worship in the Golden Age of pre-Viking Sweden. Prolonged archaeological excavation has confirmed that they were heaped over funeral pyres

race of men so resilient and self-reliant ever give of themselves sufficiently to be called true worshippers? Could a race whose poets treated their gods on occasion with such good-humoured lack of respect ever be called truly god-fearing?

We can only guess at the answers to these questions. All we know are the outward forms of their acts of worship, or some of them. But it is significant that the Norse word *blóta*, meaning 'to worship', also meant 'to honour' and 'to make sacrifice to'. It thus appears that they honoured their gods with sacrifice, and this demonstrates a less deferential attitude than the bent knee of humility. The gods were to be honoured, appeased, humoured, propitiated, but above all to be made friends with. They were powers that could make both useful allies and dangerous adversaries. They made unreliable allies, but better on your side than not.

So how did the Norsemen physically 'worship' their gods? Until comparatively recently it was believed that the Vikings worshipped in elaborate temples of timber and stone. The Norse word for temple is *hof*, and there are numerous place-names in Iceland and Norway which have the element hof, often compounded with the names of gods, as in Thórshof or Freyshof. One of the Icelandic sagas, *Eyrbyggja Saga,* contains a detailed description of such a temple built late in the ninth century by one of the first settlers in Iceland, Thórólf Mostrarskegg (father of Thorstein Cod-Biter who died and entered Helgafell), at a place called Thórsness on Snæfellsness. Thórólf was a devout man who placed all his trust in Thór; like the First Settler, Ingólf Arnarson, he had cast overboard the sacred pillars that had stood in his temple in Norway, one of which had the image of Thór carved on it, and vowed that he would settle where Thór brought them ashore. The saga continues: 'Thórólf had a large temple built there. The entrance was in one of the side walls, near the gable. Just inside the door stood the high-seat pillars, studded with nails —the so-called "divine nails"; beyond that point the whole interior of the building was a sanctuary.

'Farther inside the main temple there was a structure built rather like the chancel in churches nowadays, and in the middle of the floor there was a pedestal like an altar; on this pedestal lay a solid unjointed arm-ring weighing twenty ounces, upon which people had to swear all their oaths. This ring had to be worn by the temple-priest at all public meetings. There was a sacrificial bowl on the pedestal, too, with a sacrificial twig shaped like a priest's aspergillum, with which the blood of animals sacrificed as offerings to the gods was to be sprinkled from the bowl. The figures of the gods were arranged all round the pedestal in this chamber.

'Every farmer had to pay dues to the temple, and was also under an obligation to accompany the temple-priest to all assemblies, in the same way as constituents are nowadays obliged to support their chieftains; for his

part it was the priest's duty to maintain the temple at his own expense, as well as to hold sacrificial feasts.'

What was supposed to go on at these ceremonies was described by Snorri Sturluson in his *History of the Kings of Norway* (*Heimskringla*), in *The Saga of Hákon the Good.* He wrote about the temple rituals in Trondheim, Norway, in the middle of the tenth century:

'It was an ancient custom, when there was to be a sacrifice, that all the farmers had to attend the temple and bring with them the provisions they would need for the duration of the feast. At this feast, everyone had to join in the ale-drinking. All kinds of domestic livestock, and horses too, were slaughtered there, and all the blood that came from them was called *hlaut*; the sacrificial bowls in which the blood was kept were called *hlaut-bollar*, and the sprinklers were called *hlautteinar* (blood-twigs). The blood was used to redden all the altars and the walls of the building, both inside and out, as well as

Cult scenes from the magnificent silver Gundestrup
cauldron, found in a bog in Jutland and dating from the
first or second century BC—the Celtic Iron Age. It was
probably of Celtic workmanship, but reflects sacrificial
scenes which were part of Germanic religious rites during
the Roman period.

Left: Human sacrifice associated with a cauldron like the
Gundestrup cauldron itself, while armed men make ready
for war. The sacrifice is presumably to the War God, but
one of the mounted warriors has a helmet crest in the form
of a boar, the animal sacred to Frey.

Below left: One of the eight deities whose impassive faces
decorate the outside of the cauldron. The theme is again
that of human and animal sacrifice.

Below: The ritual slaying of a bull depicted on the base of
the cauldron. One of the attacking hounds is lying dead,
while the warrior is posed to stab the bull through the neck
from above

for sprinkling on the congregation, while the meat was cooked for people to eat. There were fires in the middle of the floor, with cauldrons suspended over them. The sacrificial cup had to be passed over the fire, and the chieftain presiding at the feast should consecrate the cup as well as all the sacrificial food. The toast of Óðin was drunk first (this was drunk to victory and the prosperity of the king), then the toast of Njörð and the toast of Frey for fruitful harvest and for peace. It was then the custom of many to drink the "chief toast", the toast to the late king; people also drank toasts in memory of their kinsmen who lay buried in mounds, and these toasts were called "remembrance".'

Both of these descriptions were written by authors with a keen interest in the customs of the pagan past. But they were writing in the thirteenth century when formal paganism had been a dead letter in Iceland for over 200 years. Earnest and detailed though these accounts are, scholars now tend to doubt their authenticity. Both descriptions are thought to derive from a note penned by Iceland's first vernacular historian, Ari Thorgilsson (Ari the Learned) early in the twelfth century. What is perhaps more remarkable is that Christian writers should have been so tolerant in their attitude to rites which were anathema to the Church elsewhere: there is only a praiseworthy effort to record, to understand and rationalize.

There are a number of farms in Iceland still called Hof or Hofstaðir (Temple Steads); until recently it was believed that they were originally all sites of temples or places of worship. The site of Thórólf Mostrarskegg's temple in *Eyrbyggja Saga* was called Hofstaðir and in 1908 another Hofstaðir, in the north of Iceland, was excavated by archaeologists. By then it was just a low ruin overgrown with grass, but the place had traditionally been associated with a temple-site. The remains of a very large building were uncovered, measuring 144 feet by 26 feet (44 m by 8 m). It was a simple construction, consisting of a long-hall with slightly curving, boat-shaped walls, and a platform running along both walls from end to end which would have been capable of seating some 150 men at tables. At one end there was a separate chamber that seemed to correspond to the 'chancel' mentioned in *Eyrbyggja Saga*. Leading off one of the side walls were two small ancillary rooms.

This building was hailed as a classic 'temple' when its discovery was first published. But further research into early house-ruins from the Viking period in Iceland suggests that it was an ordinary, albeit large, dwelling-house: a typical early long-hall with small subsidiary rooms (women's work-room, dairy, and so on) whose development in terms of domestic architecture could be traced chronologically.

There are too many references to 'public temples' in the historical literature to be completely ignored, however. *Landnámabók* (*Book of Settlements*) and other

Icelandic sources refer to solid arm-rings like the one mentioned in *Eyrbyggja Saga*, on which oaths were sworn for all business transactions and court proceedings. Early legislation required a fixed number of 'public temples' in each of the four provinces, called Quarters, and land-owning farmers were obliged to pay dues towards their upkeep, as they were later required to pay tithes to the Church.

It seems that with the passage of time, historians began to assume that the social organization of religion in pagan times resembled that of the church institutions in Christian times. These writers tended to visualize the 'temples' they had heard about in a contemporary mould. It is now generally accepted that farm-sites called Hof or Hofstaðir were actually the private houses of local chieftains who were also religious community leaders, and that they used their houses for the banquets accompanying cult celebrations and seasonal festivals.

The horned helmets so beloved of popular writers were used only for ritual and magic purposes, never in battle, where they would have been an encumbrance.
Above: Bronze amulet of a man holding a sword and two spears, and wearing a horned helmet—from a woman's grave in Uppland, Sweden. It probably represents a priest of the cult of Óðin.
Right: Sixth-century die for making helmet plates, from the island of Öland in the Baltic. The dancing figure wears a helmet whose horns terminate in birds' heads; his companion wears the mask of a wolf or bear—perhaps an echo of the 'berserks', followers of Óðin, who ran amok in battle and were impervious to weapons

The strongest evidence we have for a temple building that was specifically designed to house images of the gods and was reserved for cult activities in pagan Scandinavia is the description of the great temple at Uppsala by Adam of Bremen, and even that, with its dubious description of golden roofs, must be treated cautiously.

Acts of worship seem, then, to have taken place out of doors. Tacitus had noted that the Germans did not confine their gods within walls, but worshipped in consecrated woods and groves where the secret power of the gods was thought to reside. Most of the surviving place-names in Scandinavia which have divine associations usually compound the name of a god with natural features of the landscape like 'wood', 'hill', 'headland', 'stony outcrop', 'field', 'pasture', 'stream' and 'grove'. In the story of Frey's wooing of Gerð, as told in *Skírnismál*, Frey meets his bride in a 'windless grove'. One of the early Icelandic settlers, Thórir Snepil (Flap),

called his home Lund (Grove), and it was said of him that he held the grove sacred. Another called his home Foss (Waterfall), and held the falls similarly sacred. One chieftain is described in *Kristni Saga*, the history of the conversion of Iceland as bringing sacrifice to a rock which he regarded as the home of the family 'patron' who assured good harvests.

There were also specific areas of sanctuary, where it was forbidden to spill blood or use violence because the god was believed to be present. Ceremonial sites of various kinds were marked by *vébönd* ('sanctuary ropes').

Although most acts of worship took place in the open air in the early days, in later times there seems to have been a growing tendency to erect some kind of structure for cult purposes—not a formal temple, but a rudimentary chapel or altar of some kind. We can see this development happening through the use of the word *hörg*. Originally, it meant simply 'rocky outcrop', and

was one of the natural features that was held to be sacred to a god or earth-spirit. Later, however, it came to mean an enclosed place, and then a roofed place. It seems likely that the original 'rocky outcrop' to which sacrifices were brought was later fenced off, perhaps with 'sanctuary ropes', and then perhaps roofed over to provide shelter for carved images. Another possibility is that a cairn-like structure of stones was erected as an altar to resemble a rocky outcrop, and was called a *hörg*. Certainly, early Christian law-codes in Scandinavia forbade the veneration of hillocks and outcrops, or the building of mounds or hörgs. In one instance in the historical literature of Iceland, the hörg is portrayed as the direct antithesis to the Christian Cross. According to *Landnámabók*, one of the original settlers, a formidable matriarch called Auð the Deep-minded, was already Christian by the time she reached Iceland late in the ninth century. On a high rocky hillock near her house she erected crosses, where she performed her devotions. After her death, however, her kinsmen relapsed into paganism, and erected a hörg by the hillock, for they believed that they would enter the hill when they died.

An essential feature of the act of worship at the hörg was that it should be smeared with sacrificial blood. In the Edda poem *Hyndluljóð* (*Lay of Hyndla*), the goddess Freyja says of her favourite, Óttar:

> He raised me a hörg
> Heaped with stones—
> Now all that rock
> Is turned to fine glass;
> He reddened it anew
> With the blood of oxen;
> Óttar always had faith
> In goddesses.

The sacrificial blood that could turn stone into precious glass was also intended to refresh the god's strength. By smearing or sprinkling it on the worshippers as well, it acted as a conducting agent to let divine power flow into them. This connection was fortified by the communion of eating the flesh that had been dedicated to the god.

The hörg shrines seem to have been used chiefly for private or family worship. We can have no idea how frequently such domestic ceremonies took place, but we know that there were three major communal festivals each year. They were all associated with the seasons, and were held in the autumn, at midwinter, and at the start of summer. The autumn festival was in the nature of a harvest thanksgiving, the midwinter festival (held in the middle of January) was a Yule feast associated with the turning of the sun, and the early summer festival was designed to promote fertility and security, or in some cases to pray for victory in the Viking raids of the forthcoming summer. Judging by the Icelandic sagas,

the seasonal feasts were the high-points of the social calendar: in the crowded long-halls the ale flowed freely, young love blossomed, men reminisced and occasionally came to blows, stories of heroic exploits were remembered and repeated. The feasting could last for several days, and at the end the exhausted guests were sped on their way with gifts from the host.

But how important was the religious element? Religion was involved in public affairs, but how large a part did it play in personal life? There are instances in the sagas of men who based all their conduct on an intensely personal relationship with a god. Thórólf Mostrarskegg was one, and his patron god, Thór, smiled on him by endowing him with prosperity and great luck in fishing. Another was Hrafnkel, known as Frey's Priest, eponymous hero of *Hrafnkel's Saga*: 'Hrafnkel had one treasured possession which he held dearer than anything else he owned. It was a pale-dun stallion with a black

mane and a black stripe down the back. He called the horse Freyfaxi and gave his patron Frey a half-share in it. Hrafnkel loved this horse so passionately that he swore a solemn oath to kill anyone who rode the stallion without his permission.' When one of his shepherds was driven by force of circumstance to ride the horse that Hrafnkel had dedicated to Frey, Hrafnkel saw no alternative but to kill the boy, albeit with some compunction. From that slaying grew a chain of harsh events that humbled Hrafnkel and almost cost him his life. It was a high price to pay for loyalty to his god, but Hrafnkel would not have shrunk from it even if he had had foreknowledge of it.

Hrafnkel's Saga is a highly sophisticated work, haunted by echoes of sacrifice at many levels. Ritual human sacrifice undoubtedly took place in the Viking Age, although it was never as common as it seems to have been amongst the Germanic tribes in the days of

Below: Thingvellir (Parliament Plains) in Iceland, where the national assembly, or Althing, met in the open air every summer from 930 onwards. It always opened on a Thursday, the day sacred to Thór, when the assembly was hallowed by the leading priest-chieftain. Although there is no record of it in the sources, it is assumed that some sort of animal sacrifice also took place. Thingvellir is a huge natural arena bounded by high lava cliffs, which served as sounding boards for speakers. In the year 1000, during the great debate between pagans and Christians which preceded Iceland's peaceful conversion to Christianity, a volcano erupted in the south of Iceland, and some pagans tried to interpret this as evidence that the gods were angry; but another leading pagan priest-chieftain commented drily, pointing to the lava walls: 'At what were the gods angry when this lava ran?'

Tacitus, who recorded instances of the wholesale slaughter and dedication of prisoners of war, and Adam of Bremen noted human sacrifices at Uppsala in the eleventh century. There are also recorded instances of the Swedes sacrificing their king when crops failed.

In the Viking Age, however, human sacrifice seems to have been used only as an ultimate resort. In Iceland, in the year 1000, when the pagans and the Christians faced one another in a trial of strength at the national assembly (the Althing), the pagans decided to sacrifice two men from each Quarter in a final appeal to their gods. The sacrifice did not take place, but the Christian historian noted, somewhat primly, that 'Pagans sacrifice the worst men, hurling them over rocks or cliffs.' Sacrificial victims were also hanged, or drowned in sacred wells and morasses. There is some suggestion that in later pagan times only miscreants or slaves were sacrificed, and some of the historical sources imply that

the death-penalty for crimes was in itself a sacred rite. The author of *Eyrbyggja Saga,* who must have been an indefatigable antiquarian, says that at the assembly site near Helgafell: 'There can still be seen there the judgement circle in which men were condemned to be sacrificed; in that circle stands the Stone of Thór on which the victims' backs were broken; and you can still see traces of blood on the stone.' Presumably the purpose of this ritual was to placate the gods; but it is tempting to think that there might also have been an element of expiation involved, that the act of dedication to a god might have mitigated the crime.

Law-courts, at least in Iceland, were run by the chieftains. But Icelandic chieftains wielded not just secular power, but religious power as well. They were called *goðar* (singular *goði*) and were the men responsible for institutionalized religion. Although, etymologically, the name suggests that their priestly functions came

Above: Small copper locket containing the coiled skeleton of a snake, found in Gotland. Such amulets were believed to have magical properties
Above left: The most insistent motif in Viking art—the dragon-head. This one was found in the Oseberg ship-burial
Left: Silver arm-ring from Gotland, dating from the eleventh century, and terminating once again in dragon-heads

first, it is clear that towards the end of the pagan period the religious element was simply an adjunct of their worldly status. There is little indication in the sagas of the way they felt about their duties or their gods. We do know, however, that idolatry in the literal sense was not marked. Despite the presence of the huge statues of Óðin, Thór and Frey that Adam of Bremen noted in the temple at Uppsala, Tacitus had remarked on the fact that the Germanic tribes did not make images of the gods. There is a great deal of evidence, however, both from archaeology and the literary sources, that individual Norsemen liked to own amulets or talismans in the form of small images of the gods, or divine symbols. Some even worshipped them: one of the court poets of King Olaf Tryggvason of Norway, the evangelist of Scandinavia in the last decade of the ninth century, was accused of keeping an ivory image of Thór in his purse and worshipping it in secret. A handsome little bronze figurine of a seated bearded man, found in the north of Iceland, is believed to be a tenth-century representation of Thór. A phallic figurine found in Sweden has been identified with Frey. And innumerable amulets in the form of Thór's hammer have been found in graves.

These were simply tokens of the god in whom the owner put his trust, and may have been as perfunctory as badges for all we know. But there is one Icelandic saga in particular that illuminates a man's personal relationship with his god: the epic life-story of the warrior-poet Egil Skallagrimsson in *Egil's Saga,* which is believed to have been written by Snorri Sturluson. The Saga contains a great deal of the poetry that Egil wrote, and in particular, a long poem called *Sonatorrek (Loss of Sons),* which he composed in the year 960 or thereabouts after the death of his favourite son (he had also lost another son not long before that). Egil grew up on a farm in Iceland and was reared in the worship of Thór. He went abroad as a young man to seek fame and fortune in the royal courts of Scandinavia, where he came into contact with the aristocratic cult of Óðin. From then on, both as a Viking warrior and a poet, Egil was a confirmed Óðin-worshipper.

The loss of his son, however, shook his faith to the roots. In *Sonatorrek* he railed bitterly against the god who had betrayed his trust in him and broken the bargain they had struck through sacrifice. In the end, however, he finds a deeper understanding of the godhead, and with it a new serenity:

> High was my standing
> With the Lord of the spear;
> Confident I grew
> In trust of him;
> Until the Friend of wagons,
> The Battle-decider,
> Ripped me free
> Of friendship's ties.

I cannot then worship
Vílir's brother,
The Guardian of the gods,
With eager heart.
Yet Mímir's friend
Has given to me
Atonement for evils,
If I count my blessings.

He gave me my art,
Of flawless poetry,
Did Fenrir's Foe,
The Lord of war;
And such a mind
That I could make
Open foes
Of secret haters.

It's hard for me now.
Fenrir's sister,
Queen of the dead,
Stands on the ness.
Yet will I gladly
And in good heart,
Unrepining,
Await Hel's coming.

No translation can possibly convey the grandeur of
the poetry, the sonorous assonances and alliterations, the
starkly wrought kennings or metaphors of the original.
But in these taut stanzas, the poet's discourse with his
own soul reaches a new and sublime comprehension.
The god who had bereft him of his sons had not failed
him after all; he had given him the priceless gift of
poetry which transcended all grief, and made him
whole. There is nothing nobler in the pagan literature
of Scandinavia.

*Right: Human sacrifice, according to Tacitus, seems to
have been common during the Migration Period and the
peat-bogs of Jutland have yielded up macabre evidence of
the practice. Evidence of sacrifices of all kinds has been
found, but the most striking is the perfectly preserved
body of a man who had been ritually strangled by a rope—
the Tollund Man. On his face is a look of serene acceptance
of his fate. Women were also the victims of this practice
(inset); occasionally they were blindfolded before being
put to death*

the HeROic ethic

the legend of sigurð and the code of the warrior

The menacing face of the Germanic hero.
Left: The so-called 'Sigurð's Helmet' from a pre-Viking grave at Vendel in Sweden. Sigurð the Volsung (possibly the historical Sigebert of the Franks, who died in 575) looms out of the heroic legends that arose from the events of the Migration Period and flowered into literary form in the Icelandic Elder Edda. The cult of the hero was to colour conduct and ethics throughout the Viking Age.
Above: A tenth-century silver pendant from Östergötland in Sweden shows the characteristic helmet of the Vendel and early Viking period, with the raised eyebrow-guards and the beak on the forehead

Wealth dies,
Kinsmen die,
A man himself must likewise die;
But word-fame
Never dies
For him who achieves it well.

Wealth dies,
Kinsmen die,
A man himself must likewise die;
But one thing I know
That never dies—
The verdict on each man dead.

Hávamál (Words of the High One)

These celebrated verses are from one of the longer mythological poems in the Edda. The poem is a ninth

117

century compilation from five or six poems and fragments, consisting of 164 verses of pragmatic advice and gnomic sayings attributed to Óðin. They represent the ultimate voicing of the heroic ethic of the Viking Age.

To what extent did strictly religious concepts govern men's conduct and attitudes in the Viking Age? It is important to remember that the Viking Age was an era of tremendous social upheaval for the Scandinavians, just as much as for their 'victims'. Men were uprooted and divorced from their ancestral dead. This applied even more to the emigrants who went out to settle new lands than to the Viking warrior.

One can detect, throughout the Viking Age, a process of polarization of religious belief between Thór and Óðin, each reflecting the differing needs, vocations and circumstances of the period: Thór as the symbol of the farmer, settler and seaman, with the emphasis on sturdy self-reliance, Óðin as the symbol of the aristocratic warrior-Viking with the emphasis on guile and survival. The two polarities were not contradictory, but complementary, because in the Viking Age man was not made in God's image—gods were made in man's image.

It has already been suggested that the concept of Valhöll—the idea of an after-life of eternal feasting and fighting that warriors could look forward to—was essentially literary. It was not one, it seems, that impinged to any large extent on the day-to-day consciousness of the warrior who lived by the sword and could expect to die by it. The most remarkable aspect of the *Hávamál*, in fact, is that there is not a single mention, anywhere, of life after death, even though the words are attributed to Óðin. Apart from the strange and potent passages about Óðin hanging from the tree as a sacrifice to himself, already quoted, the *Hávamál* has nothing at all to do with mystical belief, or faith in the gods. The poem as we have it today is a compilation, but the internal evidence suggests that the original authors were Norwegians, writing in the ninth or early tenth century. Thus there is no reason to doubt that in the poem we can hear the authentic voice of the 'ordinary' Viking.

The overwhelming impression the poem gives is that of the Viking hero concerned exclusively with this world, not the next one. Immortality was a purely secular concept which depended entirely on how bravely a man faced up to inevitable death, and the only reward for that bravery was not a consolation prize with the dead in Valhöll, but the continuing esteem of the living.

Indeed, in the *Hávamál*, death was seen as the greatest evil known to man:

> The halt can ride,
> The handless can herd,
> The deaf can fight with spirit;
> A blind man is better
> Than a corpse on a pyre:
> A corpse is no good to anyone.

Right: Everywhere they went, the Vikings took their heroic legends with them. This tenth-century cross in the churchyard at Halton, in Lancashire, England, depicts a number of scenes from the story of Sigurð and how he slew the dragon Fáfnir. Most of the panels are now extremely worn
Below: The face of the Viking hero—pragmatic, moustached, determined—on silver pendants from Gotland dating from the Viking period
Bottom: Similar faces on Viking coins found in Britain

Survival was the first imperative and, to that end, the *Hávamál* gives a great deal of prudent, pragmatic, sometimes cynical advice for the traveller, the stranger, the rootless man: in effect, the Viking. Look carefully round doorways before you walk in. Keep your mouth shut and your eyes and ears open. Use your wits. Don't get drunk. Don't eat too much. Don't pick a fight unnecessarily—but don't run from one if it is forced on you. Don't overstay your welcome. Always keep your weapons within reach. Get up early. Don't be too clever. Cultivate your friends with gifts. And keep a clear head about women: 'Praise a wife when she has been cremated . . . a virgin after she has been married.'

The emphasis on the cultivation of friendship is interesting. This is the ethos of the mercenary band aboard a Viking ship, where one's life depended upon one's shipmates. It is very different from that of the landed man with his network of kinships and family ties. Wealth was not to be hoarded for one's heirs, but spent upon one's friends: a cynic might suggest that this was buying friendship. But it should not be done too extravagantly:

> No need to give
> Too much to a man—
> A little can buy much thanks;
> With half a loaf
> And a half-drained jug
> I often won me a friend.

A gift always looks to its return. Friendship, to the Viking, was a self-seeking thing, a matter of expedience; and a false friend should be treated with guile. In the same way, sacrifice to a god was a matter of exchanging gifts, of buying his friendship. In return for the gift, whether it was an offering of food, or the gift of a horse or even a son, the god was expected to show the donor some favour. And when the god failed, he could be abandoned as a false friend, just as Egil Skallagrimsson almost abandoned Óðin when his sons were killed.

For every Egil Skallagrimsson who committed himself to Óðin, however, there were as many who committed themselves to no god at all. They were the men who believed only in their own might and main—at least according to the literary sources. The semi-legendary Danish King, Hrothulf, who if he ever lived at all must have ruled Denmark in the sixth century and was remembered in *Beowulf* as well as by Saxo Grammaticus, was idealized in the Icelandic *Saga of Hrólf Kraki* as the hero who despised all pagan practices and never made sacrifice to the gods. He and his champions had nothing but contempt for Óðin, yet in the saga they died a glorious death, defending themselves against overwhelming odds, each vying with the other to die the most nobly. And although the first settler of Iceland, Ingólf Arnarson, was a devout Norwegian who sacrificed carefully to the gods, his foster-brother, Hjörleif, who sailed with him to Iceland, refused to have any truck with the gods, although he apparently paid the penalty when he was killed by his slaves soon after he landed in Iceland.

The aristocrats might like to model themselves upon Óðin, or see themselves in his image as subtle, ruthless, cunning and sophisticated. The farmers might look to Thór as their model: doughty, bluff, stolid and strong. But the gods of the Norse pantheon could never provide absolute models for human behaviour. Like the classical gods, they were both superhuman and subhuman. The real models of conduct for Viking society were the heroes (some of them semi-divine) of ancient literature. It is in the heroic lays of the Edda, rather than in the mythological lays, that we can see the mould in which the Norsemen cast themselves, the concepts which governed the conduct of their lives.

There were four main concepts that affected everything they did and thought: the concept of kinship and loyalty, the concept of honour, the concept of vengeance, and that of Fate. And of these it was the idea of Fate that played the largest part.

Fate was the great leveller. Gods and men, heroes and cowards, rich men and poor, all were equally helpless before it. Belief in the implacable power of Fate was probably stronger than belief in any god throughout the Viking Age. The Norns seem to have been a literary attempt to personalize the power of Fate, but they never achieved any stature as deities. If a man were fated to die, there was nothing to be done about it, except to die well. None could escape destiny, however evil or undeserved; it was the way in which a man met his death that counted. Often this Fate seemed to be spun from a hideously complicated web of kinships and loyalties, of impossible choices involving personal honour and revenge, but it was inescapable.

All these concepts are displayed with stark power in the cycle of sixteen lays in the *Elder Edda* on the Brynhild-Sigurð-Guðrún theme—perhaps the most celebrated theme in all heroic literature. These lays, some of them very short, do not in themselves form a coherent story. They are highlights of a story, vivid glimpses of drama rather than connected narrative. The protagonists in the drama can all be associated with historical figures from the period of the great Germanic migrations during the fourth, fifth and sixth centuries AD, but they were not contemporaries, and could not have been involved with one another in any way. Nor were the poets concerned with the political or military significance of the great tribal leaders like Ermanaric the Goth (died 375), Gunnar the Burgundian (died 437), Attila the Hun (died 453), and Sigebert the Frank (died 575). These characters were fused into a narrative on a purely personal level, ignoring their massive wars in Europe and concentrating only on the fierce human dramas involved in their

The story of Sigurð the Dragon-Slayer is told in a series of carved roundels on the portals of the twelfth-century stave church at Hylestad, Norway.
Above: Regin the smith reforges the broken sword that had belonged to Sigurð's father; after reforging, the sword was able to split the anvil.
Right: Sigurð, lying in the shallow pit he had dug in the track which the dragon Fáfnir used, attacks the dragon from below, and kills it

relationships with one another, and with their wives, lovers and kinsmen.

This is the story of the Volsungs (or, in later German poetry, the Nibelungs of the thirteenth-century *Nibelungenlied* we have already mentioned). It is thought that the elements of the story reached Scandinavia by AD 800, and formed the basis for the composition of some of the lays enshrined in the *Elder Edda*. But to see how they all connect up, we have to turn to Snorri Sturluson again, and to the long treatise he wrote on poetic diction, called the *Skáldskaparmál*.

In Snorri's Edda, the seeds are sown with a hoard of gold that has been accursed. It had been plundered by Loki, on Óðin's behalf, from a dwarf called Andvari to pay compensation for a man they had slain. The man's brothers, Fáfnir and Regin, demanded a share of the gold from their father, but when this was refused, they slew him. The brothers then fell out over the division of the spoils, and Fáfnir refused to let his brother have a share of it and drove him away. He then changed himself into a dragon and made himself a lair from which to guard the gold.

Meanwhile the other brother, Regin, became a great smith in exile, and fostered a likely young hero called Sigurð the Volsung to be the instrument of his vengeance on his brother. He forged a fine sword for him, which was so sharp that it could slice through a wisp of wool floating downstream in a river, and he advised the young hero to dig a pit in the track which Fáfnir used and to attack him from below. Sigurð followed his advice, and slew the dragon. Regin now told him that it was his brother he had slain, and in compensation for his death he ordered Sigurð to roast the dragon's heart, while he himself drank the dragon's blood (this, it turned out, was to enable him to understand the speech of birds and animals). Sigurð did as he was bidden, but he burnt his finger on the roasting heart and licked it,

Above left: Sigurð roasts the dragon's heart while Regin sleeps, and burns his thumb on it; on tasting the dragon's blood on his injured finger, Sigurð gains the power to understand the speech of birds, and learns from them that Regin is planning treachery
Above: Sigurð kills the treacherous Regin with his sword
Above right: Two scenes from a later stage of the Sigurð epic cycle. After Sigurð's death at the hands of his brothers-in-law, Gunnar and Högni, they alone know the secret of where the Treasure of the Nibelungs is hidden. Atli (Attila the Hun) captures and tries to get the secret from them. In the scene on the left, which comes from another church portal, Atli's men cut Högni's living heart from his breast at Gunnar's insistence, so that Gunnar should be the only man left alive who knows the secret. Gunnar now refuses to divulge the secret, and is hurled into a snake pit, in the scene on the right, where he dies playing the harp with his feet

thereby tasting the blood from the heart. Thus Sigurð, too, gained the power to understand the speech of birds and from them he learned that Regin was planning treachery. Sigurð then slew Regin and took the hoard of gold for himself.

In his wanderings, Sigurð penetrated an enchanted wall of flame to rescue a Valkyrie called Sigrdrífa (or in some sources Brynhild), who adumbrates the theme of the events that follow.

Sigurð made his way to the realm of King Gjúki. The king had two sons called Gunnar and Högni, and a beautiful daughter called Guðrún. Sigurð married Guðrún Gjúkadóttir, and swore a pact of blood-brotherhood with her brothers. Then Sigurð accompanied the brothers on a visit to Atli (Attila), King of the Huns, for Gunnar wanted to marry Atli's sister, Brynhild. Brynhild lived in a bower encircled with a wall of flame, and had vowed never to marry anyone but the hero who dared to ride through the flames to her. Gunnar's horse refused, so Sigurð rode through the flames on his own horse, in Gunnar's guise, and spent the night with Brynhild with his sword lying chastely between them. When they parted, he gave her a ring from the gold-hoard, and she gave him a ring in exchange. Sigurð now changed places with Gunnar again, and Brynhild went home to Gjúki's kingdom as Gunnar's wife.

All would have gone well had Guðrún and Brynhild not fallen out. Washing their hair in the river one day, Brynhild waded farther out into the stream, saying that she did not care to have her own hair soiled by water from Guðrún's hair, for she had the better husband. Guðrún retorted that her own husband, Sigurð, had proved his worth by killing Fáfnir and Regin, to which Brynhild replied that only Gunnar had dared to ride through the wall of flames to reach her. Guðrún laughed, promptly showing her the ring she had given Sigurð

after the bridal night, and Brynhild fell silent. Brynhild went home and urged Gunnar and Högni to kill their blood-brother, saying that Sigurð had betrayed Gunnar's trust on the bridal night and had made love to her. And so, reluctantly, they killed Sigurð and took the hoard of gold. But Brynhild, her vengeance achieved and her honour assuaged, committed suicide and was laid with Sigurð on his funeral pyre.

With Sigurð dead, his widow Guðrún married Brynhild's brother, Atli the Hun, and had two children by him. Atli was jealous of his new brothers-in-law, Gunnar and Högni, with their hoard of gold, and invited them to a feast. Guðrún warned her brothers that the invitation was a trap, but Gunnar insisted on accepting it, seeing it as a challenge to his courage and his manhood. Before they set off, however, the brothers hid the treasure in the Rhine. No sooner had they arrived at Atli's citadel than they were seized. Gunnar was offered his life if he would tell Atli where the gold was hidden, but Gunnar made an extraordinary counter-demand: before he would reveal the whereabouts of the gold, he must first be given his brother's heart. His captors tried to deceive him by bringing the bloody, palpitating heart of someone else, but Gunnar knew that it could not be Högni's heart because it trembled, and that was something that Högni's heart had never done. So they cut open Högni's breast and tore his living heart out—and Högni laughed as they did so. Now, in triumph, Gunnar told Atli why he had made this macabre demand: for now, and only now, Gunnar could be sure that the secret was safe, as he was the only man left alive who knew it, and he would never tell. Atli ordered him to be thrown alive into a snake-pit, despite the pleas of Guðrún. Gunnar died nobly, his hands bound but playing his harp with his feet and defying death to the last.

Now Guðrún prepared a terrible vengeance for her

brothers. She killed her two sons by Atli, and from their skulls she fashioned drinking bowls set in gold and silver. At the funeral feast for her brothers, she gave her husband mead mixed with the blood of his sons to drink, and their roasted hearts to eat. Then, when he was drunk, she told him what she had done, and that night she stabbed Atli to death and set fire to his citadel, so that the entire royal household were burnt to death.

Historically, there is a tenuous connection between Attila the Hun (Atli) and Gundicarius (Gunnar) the Burgundian: it was Attila's armies that killed Gundicarius and routed his army, in 437. Sixteen years later, Attila married a German wife called Hildico (Kriemhilde in *Nibelungenlied*). On the morning after his wedding night he was found dead in bed in a pool of blood, after a haemorrhage. It seems to have been a natural death, but soon the story got around that he had been murdered by his bride.

In the final act of this dynastic drama, Guðrún had married again. Her third husband was called Jónakr, and by him she had two sons, Hamðir and Sörli. Meanwhile, Guðrún's daughter by Sigurð (her first husband), had been married to King Jörmunrekk (Ermanaric the Goth), and was later killed by her husband, who had her trampled to death by horses on suspicion of having an affair with her step-son. Guðrún the avenger now incited her sons, Hamðir and Sörli, to take vengeance for their half-sister.

They both knew that any attack on Jörmunrekk would mean their own deaths as well. They reminded their mother of the bloodshed in the family: Guðrún's brothers dead, her first two sons dead. But they did not shirk the terrible imperatives of duty, and rode off to their doom. They effected entry to Jörmunrekk's hall where he sat feasting amongst his followers. They fought their way to Jörmunrekk, and cut off his arms and legs, but in the end they were overcome and stoned to death:

> We have fought right well,
> We stand on slaughtered Goths,
> Surmounting the sword-weary dead
> Like eagles on a bough.
> We have won good fame
> Whether we die now or tomorrow:
> No man outlives the evening
> After the Norns' decree.

The heroic ethic of the Brynhild-Sigurð-Guðrún cycle is a tragic one, born of fatalism and stoicism. These themes recur over and over again in the Icelandic Sagas, where farmers were forced by circumstance and social convention to become heroes, or else die unsung. In the Norse world, the family was all-important, and the ties of kinship imposed powerful demands as well as conferring strength and support. Any injury to one's kin

was an injury to oneself and 'honour' demanded that the slight be removed, either by bloody revenge or by proper compensation. The laws actually expected vengeance: a man's good name could only be protected by successful retaliation. Norse society placed overwhelming importance on personal and family prestige, so every man had to be alert to anything that might threaten it. Vengeance was obligatory—whatever the cost might be to oneself.

Sometimes the demands of kinship clashed with the demands of honour, and that was where the real tragedy lay. There was nothing in the laws that covered disputes between kinsmen; at such times the individual had only his own judgment to fall back on, and was forced to make the choice between two evils that is the stuff of heroic drama.

For such situations, the *Hávamál* had no advice to offer. Moderation was all very well. Survival was all very well. But there were times when such considerations had to be ignored. The Norse ideal was a man of open, generous disposition, a man imbued with qualities of compassion and kindness, not ruthless but firm and fair, even-tempered but capable of passion, physically accomplished and strong in a fight, but not a bully. Such was the ideal man of honour. But when the die was cast, when circumstances and cruel fate drew him into a situation which he could not avoid without losing honour, when he was agonizingly trapped between duty and emotion, there was no running away. If he had to kill, he killed, and if he had to die, he died well, like Högni, laughing at death itself.

It was a harsh and inescapable ethic. But it was an ethic that bound the gods as well. The gods, too, would have to face their deaths one day, and however remote they might seem from the real world of men, in the end they faced their own fate with the same stoicism, the same heroic fatalism, as the best of heroes.

Right: Seventh-century Vendel helmet from Sweden. The cap is of iron and a bronze crest runs down to join the nose-guard, a pattern that might well derive from Roman models. This awesome object reflects both the vigour and the mystery of Scandinavia, qualities that found expression in the cult of the hero and his gods

BIBLIOGRAPHY

Branston, B., *Gods of the North*, Thames and Hudson, London 1955; Vanguard Press, New York 1955.

Davidson, H. R. Ellis, *Scandinavian Mythology*, Paul Hamlyn, Feltham 1969.

Dronke, U. (Ed.), *The Poetic Edda*, Oxford University Press, London and New York 1969.

Jones, G., *History of the Vikings*, Oxford University Press, London 1973 and New York 1968.

Kristjánsson, J., *Icelandic Sagas and Manuscripts*, Saga Publishing, Reykjavik 1970.

Magnusson, M., *Viking Expansion Westwards*, Bodley Head, London 1973; Walck, Henry Z., New York 1973.

Turville-Petre, G., *Myth and Religion of the North*, Weidenfeld and Nicholson, London 1964.

Wilson, D. M. and Foote, P. G., *Viking Achievement*, Sidgwick and Jackson, London 1971; Praegger, New York 1970.

Wilson, D. M. and Klindt-Jensen, O., *Viking Art*, George Allen and Unwin, London 1966; Cornell University Press, Ithaca, N.Y. 1966.

INDEX

Page references to illustrations are printed in *italic* type

Abalus 10
Adam of Bremen 39, 58, 61, 69, 76, 109, 112, 113
Æsir 49, 55, 56, 62, 70, 74, 75, 79
Agriculture 9, 14
Alcuin 22, 26
Alfred the Great 29, 36, 38
All-Father 46, 49, 56
Alphabet 13
Álfheim (Elfworld) 92
Amber 9, 11, *69*
Amulet, bronze 108; gold *72-3*; gold foils 76; locket *113*; mould *44*; silver *70, 71*
Andalusia 14
Andvari 122
Angles 14, 74
Anglo-Saxons 18, 36, 41, 58, 60, 65
Anglo-Saxon Chronicle 26, 27, 36
Angrboða (Distress-Bringer) 80, 96
Anskar 38
Anthropology 31
Aral Sea 27
Archaeology 10, 12, 16, 17, 27, 28, 31, 61, 99, 105
Arctic Circle 10
Arctic Stone Age 10, 11
Ari Thorgilsson 108
Arm-ring, silver *112*
Armagh Abbey 36
Art 10, 11, 12, 17, 40
Ása 24

Ásaland (Asia) 56
Asatru 55
Ásgarð 48, 49, 51, 56, 58, 63, 70, 75, 79, 80, 82, 92, 96
Asia Minor 12
Ásmund Atlason 98
Áss 55
Atlantic 30, 31
Atli 123; *see also* Attila
Attila the Hun 14, 120, 123, 124
Auð the Deep-minded 110
Aureus 14
Axe, Mammen *31*

Baffin Island 41
Baldur 49, 52, 53, 75, 82, 83, 84
Baltic 14, 18, 39, 74
Baptism 36, 38, 39
Bard of Snaefellsness 91
Barri (Barley) 77
Battle-Axe people 10
Bede, the Venerable 60
Belgae 13
Beowulf 13, 14, 119
Bifröst 48, 51
Bird-clasp *63*
Bird-mask *62*
Birka 28, 38
Black Sea 21, 27
Blóta 106
Boar 76
Boats 17, 18, *19*, 97, 98; *see also* Ships
Breiðablik (Broad Splendour) 82
Bremen 36

Brian Boru 29
Bridle-mount *16, 102*
Brísing treasure 76
Britain 10, 14
Bronze 17
Bronze Age 11, 12, 56
Bronze matrix 75
Brooches *17, 93, 102-3*
Buddha 16, *19*
Búri 47
Brunhilda 90
Brynhild 90, 123
Burial customs 11, 13, 14, *14*, *94-5*, 96, 97, 102, 103; *see also* Funerals, Graves
Burial mounds; Uppsala *104-5*

Caesar 57
Cairns 92
Canute 29; *see also* Knút
Cart from Oseberg ship *98-9*
Caspian Sea 27
Celts 12, 13
Charlemagne 27, 35, 36, 38
Chartres 30
China 27
Christ 38, 74
Christianity 30, 31, 35, 36, 40, 44, 49, 53, 56, 62, 74, 84, 90, 92, 105
Church 21, 38, 39, 56, 108
Cimbri 13, 61
Climate 12, 31
Clonmacnoise 40
Clontarf, Battle of, 29, 88

Codex Regius 44
Cog 36
Coins 21, 27, *118*; Arabic 28
Columbus, Christopher 31
Communion 38
Constantinople 21, 27, 28
Copper 11
Cosmology 44, 46
Cross, Christian 110; Halton *119*; Kirkby Stephen *82*
Crozier, bronze *33*

Danegeld 39
Danelaw 29, 38
Danube 12
Dark Elves 92
De Bello Gallico 57
Democracy 40
Denmark 11, 14, 18, 29, 35, 36, 38, 39, 56, 58, 61, 92
Diet 9
Dís 90
Disablót 90
Disir 87, 90, 91
Divinities 55
Dnieper 27
Dofri 91
Doomsday 53
Dorchester 27
Dorset, Sheriff of 26
Dovrefell 91
Draupnir 77, 83
Druids 57
Dublin 29
Dwarves 58, 65, 69, 87, 92, *93*

Earth Goddess 57
Economy 14
Edda, Elder 44, 46, 61, 70, 80, 120, 122
Edda manuscript *47*
Edda, Poetic 30, 44, 46, 70, 90, 95, 120
Edmund of East Anglia 36
Egil Skallagrimsson 113, 119
Egil's Saga 36, 113
Elbe 14
Elli 72
Elves 87, 92
Emigration 34
England 18, 21, 27, 29, 33, 38, 39, 60
Eric Blood-Axe 65
Ermanaric the Goth 14, 120
Ethelred the Unready 29
Europe 9, 13, 27, 39, 120
Exploration 41
Eyrbyggja Saga 102, 106, 108

Fáfnir 122
Family and kinship 124
Fárbanti (Cruel Smiter) 80
Faroes 30, 39
Fate 49, 88, 120, 124
Feasts 110
Fenrir 49, 50, 51, *51*, 58, 80
Figurines, amber *69*; bronze *13*, *56*, *57*, *59*, *75*
Fimbul 50
Fire Giants 50, 51
Flateyjarbók 91
Fleets 14, *26*; see also Ships
Foils, gold *76*
Foss 109
France 18, 30
Franks 14
Frey 12, 51, 56, 57, 69, 74, 75, 76, 77, 83, 103, 109, 118
Freyfaxi 76, 111
Freyshof 106
Freyja 74, *74*, 76, 80, 90, 110
Frigedæg 65
Frigg 65, 82, 83
Frisians 14
Frjá 65
Frost Giantess 75
Frost Giants 47, 51, 77, 83
Funerals 11, 12, 36, 38, 83; *see also* Burial customs
Furs 17, 28
Fylgjur (fetches) 90

Ganger-Rolf 29
Garm 58, 96
Gates of Hel 84
Gaul 14, 57
Gautar; see Goutoi
Geats 13
Geographica 10
Gerð (Field) 77, 109
Germania 57, 74
Germans 13, 53, 56, 57, 61, 74, 109, 111, 113, 120
Giantland 75, 77, 80, 81, 83
Ginnungagap (The Great Void) 44, 47, 95
Gisli's Saga 97
Gísli Súrsson 97

Gjöll (Howling) 88
Gjöll Bridge 96
Gjúki 123
Glass 17
Gods 11, 87, 90, 109, 118, 124
Gokstad ship 22, *24*, 25, *25*, 35
Gold 11, 17, 122
Golden Age 52, 88
Golden Forelock 83
Göll (Screaming) 88
Gorm the Old 38
Goths 13
Goutoi 13
Graves 12, 14, *15*, 96
'Great Heathen Horde' 29
Greece 12
Greenland 21, 30, 31, *34–5*, 41
Guðrún Gjúkadóttir 123, 124
Gullinbursti (Gold-Bristed) 76
Gundestrup Cauldron *106–7*
Gundicarius (Gunnar) the Burgundian 14, 120, 123
Gungnir 62
Gunnar of Hlíðarendi 103, *123*
Gylfaginning (*The Beguiling of Gylfi*) 46, 48, 56, 58, 60, 75
Gylfi 46

Hadding 102
Hall of Death 96
Hall of Hel 84
Hall of Siða 90, 91
Hamburg 38
Hamðir 124
Hammer; see Thór
Hánga-týr 58
Hanseatic sea-routes 36
Harald Blue-Tooth 38
Harald Fine-Hair 24, 34, 91, 92
Harald Gormsson 92
Harness mounts *64–5*
Hávamal 61, 117, 118, 119, 124
Hebrideans 30
Hedeby 38
Heimdall 51, 80, 82, 83
Heimskringla (*History of the Kings of Norway*) 92, 106
Hel 80, 83, 95, 102
Helgafell 102, 113
Helgi the Lean 74
Helgö 16
Heligoland 10
Helmet, Vendel *20*, *116*, *125*
Helmet plate *59*, *62*, *109*
Hel-shoes 97
Helway 96
Hengist 60
Hermóð the Valiant 83, 84, 96
Hildico 124
History of the World 61
Hjörleif 120
Hjortspring boat 18
Hlaut 106
Hlautbollar 106
Hlauteinar (blood twigs) 106
Hlökk (Shrieking) 88
Höð 83
Hof 106
Hofstaðir 108
Hogback tomb *49*
Högni 123, *123*, 124
Hörg 109, 110

Horsa 60
Horn of Plenty, *89*
Horse-collar, Mammen *52*
Hrafnkel 76, 111
Hrafnkel's Saga 76, 111
Hringhorni 83
Hrothulf 119
Hrúmfaxi (Frosty-Mane) 47
Hrungnir 70
Hugi 72
Huginn 63
Humber 38
Hygelac of the Geats 14
Hýmir 72
Hyndluljóð (*Lay of Hyndla*) 110
Hyrrokin 83

Ibn Fadlan 99, 100
Ibn Rustah 98
Iceland 21, 30, 31, 39, 41, 58, 65, 74, 76, *86–7*, 90, 91, 92, 98, *110–11*, 113, 120
Icelandic sagas 31
Idunn 75
Indra 69
Ingolf Arnarson 92, 106, 119
Institutions 40
Iona 27
Ireland 21, 27, 29, 36, 88
Iron Age 12, 14, 16, 17
Isle of Man 99
Italy 12, 14
Ivory 17

Jan Mayen Island 41
Jarrow 27
Jelling 38
Jelling stone *41*
Jónakr 124
Jörð 69
Jordanes 13
Jörmunrekk 124
Jötenheim 48, 49
Justice 40
Jutes 14
Jutland 10, 11, 18, 61, 114

Kiev 27
Killer-Hrapp 103
Kirkwell 30
Knörr 25, 26, 27
Knút (Canute) 38, 39, 40
Kormak's Saga 92
Kristnes 74
Kristni Saga 109
Kvalsund ship 18
Kvasir 64

Lake Mälaren 16
Landnámabók (*Book of Settlements*) 98, 108
Landvættir (land-spirits) 87, 92
Lapps 17
Law 40
Law-courts 113
Laxdæla Saga 103
Lays 44, 46, 76
Light Elves 92
Limerick 29
Lindisfarne 22, *22–3*, 26
Literature 41, 114
Logi 71

Loki 49, 51, 58, 79, 80, 82, 122
Lokasenna (*Loki's Taunting*) 80
Lombards 13
Long Serpent 35
Louis the Pious 38
Lund (Grove) 109
Lur 12, *13*

Magic 12
Magni (Might) 70
Mammen axe *31*; horse-collar *42–3*
Mannus 48
Mars 57, 58
Marseilles 9
Mediterranean 13, 18
Megingjarðar 69
Memorial picture-stone *12*
Mercenaries 28
Merchant shipping 36; see also Ships
Mercury 57, 61
Metallurgy 28, 34
Miðgarð (Middle Enclosure) 48, 82
Miðgarðsorm 49
Migrations 14
Mímir 62
Missionaries 39
Mistletoe 83
Mjöllnir 70, 71, 80
Muninn 63
Múspell 47, 51, 82
Mythology 44, 49, 56, 57, 61, 69, 74, 76, 92, 95, 117

Nabidh 100
Naglfari 50
Nanna 83
Navigation 25
Neolithic Age 10
Nerthus 57, 74, 75
Newfoundland 25, 31
Nibelungenlied 90, 122
Nibelungs 122
Níðhögg 49
Niflheim or Niflhel *44–5*, 47, 95, 96
Njál's Saga 74, 103
Njörð 57, 74, 75, 76, 80, 108
Nóatún (Anchorage) 75
Normans 30, 35
Normandy 30, 39
Norns 49, 87, 88, 120
Norse 12, 14, 27, 30, 40, 53, 65, 79, 120
North Africa 14
North America 21, 30, 41
Northumberland 22, 27, 29, 38
Norway 10, 18, 22, 25, 30, 35, 38, 39, 56, 65, 76, 91, 92
Novgorod 27, 28
Nydam boat 18

Ocean 48, 49, 50, 69, 72, 75
Óðin 12, 16, 46, 47, 48, 49, 50, 51, *54–5*, 56, 58, 60, *60*, 61, 62, 75, 77, *78*, 79, 80, 88
Óður 58
Olaf (Elf of Geirstadir) 92
Olaf Haraldsson (Olaf the Stout) 39

Olaf Tryggvason 35, 39, 113
Olaf of Vestfold 25
On the Ocean 9
Öre 14
Orkneys 10, 27, 30, 39
Orosius 61
Oseberg ship burial 22, 24, *24–5*, 98; bucket *101*; cart *32, 98–9*; dragon-head *81, 112*; head-post *52*; sledge *53*
Oslo 22
Ostrogoths 14
Otherworld 12, 49, 50, 52, 58, 62, 77, 80, 82, 83, 95, 96, 97, 102
Óttar 110

Paganism 30, 36, 46, 56, 74, 92, 108, 110, 114, 119
Pendant, silver *83, 117, 118*
Picts 27
Pliny the Elder 13
Poetry 46, 77, 89, 113
Population 34
Portland 26
Priests 39, 40
Ptolemy 13
Pytheas 9, 10, 12, 13

Quarters 108
Queen of the Dead 95

Ragnar Hairybreeks 36
Ragnarök 49, 58, 64, 72, 77, 80, 82, 92
Ratatosk 49
Red Indians 31
Regin *120, 122, 122*, 123
Religion 12, 56, 75
Rhine 12, 57, 123
Rhône 61
Ribe 38
Ringerike style 40
Ring, gold *103*
Ring of the Nibelung 90
Rock carvings 11, 18, 56; hunting *10*; ship *11*; sky-god *58–9*; warriors and bull *11*
Rock Giant 82, 83, 92
'Rollo' 29; *see also* Ganger-Rolf
Romans 13, 14, 58, 61
Roskilde Fjord 25, 36
Rurik 28
Rus 27, 28
Russia 21, 27, 39, 102
Russian Primary Chronicle 27

Sacrifice 39, 57, 61, 92, 102, 108
Saga of Hrólf Kraki 119
Saga of St Olaf 38, 39
Sagas 31
St Augustus 36
St Magnus Cathedral 30
St Olaf *38*
Saxo Grammaticus 119
Saxons 14
Scandinavia 9, 10, 11, 12, 13, 17, 27, 30
Scilly Isles 39
Scotland 21, 30
Scyldings 16, 56
Scythia 12
Serpent 57
Sessrúmnir (Roomy) 76
Shetland 10, 27, 30, 39
Ships 11, 17, 18, *29*, 30, 35, 36
Shrine of the Crozier 40
Sibyl's Prophecy, The (Völuspá) 49
Siegfried 90
Sif 80
Sigebert 90, 120
Sigrdrífa (Victory-Giver) 90, 123
Sigurð 90, *120, 121, 122, 122*, 123
Sigyn 82
Silver 17
Skaði (Harm) 75, 76, 80
Skáldskaparmál 122
Skálholt 30
Skínfaxi (Shining-Mane) 47
Skírnir (The Bright One) 77
Skirnismál 71, 109
Skjöld (Shield) 16, 56
Skögul (Raging) 88
Skuld 88
Sky-deities 56
Slaves 75, 98
Sleetcold 96
Sleipnir *78*, 80, 83, 96, *97*
Smolensk 27
Snæfellsness 106
Snorri Sturluson 46, 47, 48, 56, 58, 63, 70, 76, 79, 82, 92, 113
Social organization 13
Sogne Fjord *28*, 66–7
Sonattorrek (Loss of Sons) 113
Sorcery 62
Sörli 124
Sow 76
Spain 12, 14
Spear *31*
Spitzbergen 41
Stave-church 30, *37*
Stern 99

Stone Age 10
Stone of Thór 113
Strabo of Pontus 13
Suiones 13, 14
Sun *46*, 47, 57
Surt 47
Surtsey 47
Survival 119
Sutton Hoo 18
Suttung 65
Svaðilfari (Hazard-Farer) 82
Svein Ásleifsson 30
Svein Fork-Beard 29, 38
Svíar of Uppland 13, 16
Sweden 14, 16, 27, 38, 39, 61, 69, 76, 112
Sword *31*

Tacitus 13, 18, 48, 57, 61, 74, 109, 112
Tale of Thiðrandi and Thórhill 90
Tapestry, Skog Church *36*, 54–5
Temples 106, 108
Terra Mater 57
Teutones 10, 13
Thangbrand 74
Thingvellir *110–11*
Thiðrandi 90, 91
Thjálfi 72
Thjazi 75
Thökk 84
Thór 12, 36, 51, *54–5*, 56, 65, *68*, 70, 71, 80, 82, 103
Thór's hammer *70, 71, 82*
Thorfinn Karlsefni 31
Thorgrim 97
Thorhall the Prophet 91
Thórir Snepil 109
Thórólf Mostrarskegg 106, 108
Thorshof 106
Thórsness 106
Thorstein Cod-Biter 102
Thrym 80
Thrym's Lay (þrymskviða) 80
Thule *8–9*, 10
Thyri 38
Timber 17, 30
Tin 9, 11
Tiwaz 58
Tollund man 61, *114*
Tombstone, St Paul's Cathedral *40–41*
Trade routes 13, 14, 27
Treasure 11, 16, 22
Trolls 87
Trondheim 106

Tune ship 22, 25
Tvisto 48
Tyr 58, *58–9*

Uppsala 39, 40, 61, 69, 76, *104–5*, 109, 112, 113
Urðr 88
Urn, cremation *76–7*
Útgarðar-Loki 70, 71, 72

Valhöll 64, 65, 90, *96*, 102, 118
Valkyries 64, 83, 87, 88, *88, 89, 90*, 123
Vandals 14
Vanir 49, 56, 62, 74
Varangian Guard 28, 30
Vengeance 124
Verðandi 88
Vestein 97
Vestfold 25
Vik 26
Viking Age 11, 21, 79
Viking Ship Museum 22, 25
Vínland 31
Visigoths 14, 90
Vistula 14
Volga 27, 98, 102
Volkhov 27
Volsung 122
Völuspá (The Sibyl's Prophecy) 43, 46, 49, 53, 62, 88, 92, 96

War of the Irish & the Foreigner 22, 29
Waterford 29
Weathervane *26*
Well of Fate 51, 87
Weser 36
Wexford 29
White God 82
Wicklow 29
William 30
Winchester style 40
Wodan (Woden, Wotan) 60, 69
World Serpent 50, 51, 69, 72, 80
World Tree; *see* Yggdrasil
Wyrd (Fate) 88

Yggdrasil 48, 49, 51, 61, 62, 87
Ýmir 47, 48, 92
Ynglings 16, 56
Yngvi-Frey 16, 56
York 65
Yule feast 110

Zeus 58

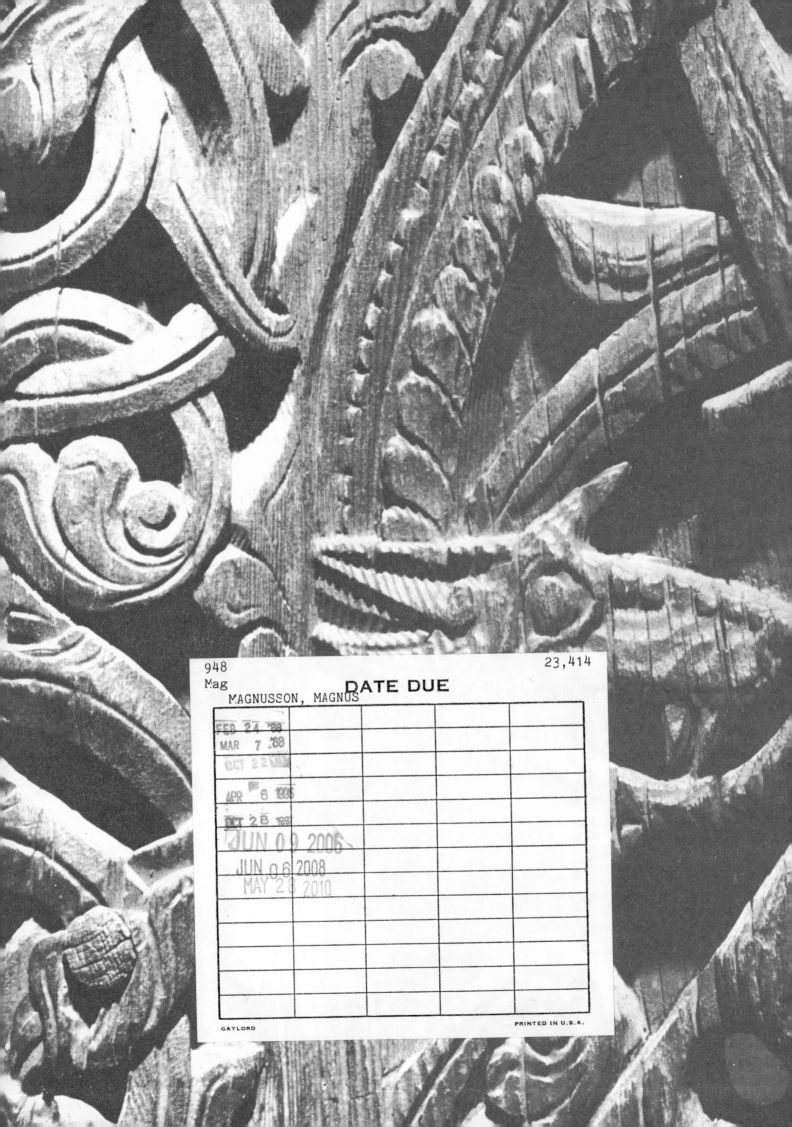